JESUS WAS
& IS ALWAYS
WITH ME

JESUS WAS
& IS ALWAYS
WITH ME
THROUGHOUT MY LIFE

EUGENE MCCANN

 AuthorCentrix

Printed in the United States of America
ISBN 978-1-64133-339-9 (sc)
ISBN 978-1-64133-338-2 (hc)
ISBN 978-1-64133-337-5 (e)

Library of Congress Control Number: 2018931258

Non-Fiction / Biography & Memoir
18.04.20

AuthorCentrix
25220 Hancock Ave #300,
Murrieta, CA 92562

www.authorcentrix.com

"And his fame went throughout all Syria: and they brought unto him all sick people that were taken with divers' diseases and torments, and those which were possessed with devils, and those which were lunatic, and those that had the palsy; and he healed them."
Matthew 4:24

"We must love ourselves and know that we do count. We do matter, no matter what. Whatever happened to us, does not define us. I cannot stress that enough." - *Eugene McCann*

Acknowledgements

I would like to express my special thanks to Deanna McCann, my lovely wife, who has been with me throughout the writing of this book. Her presence in my daily life is a great blessing, and I love her very much.

My deep gratitude goes to Father George Farrell, who helped restore my health, and for supporting me to write this book. He showed me where to begin, and I am forever indebted for his assistance.

Abbot Notker Wolf, a dear friend of mine, I will always remember him and miss him profoundly. He was a great friend of mine who has left me with even much greater memories.

I shall acknowledge the rest as they all have been a major part of writing this book. They all have been a wonderful inspiration to me, and there is not enough room to mention all these awesome people and friends:

Eileen Molnari, Richard Emerson, Father. Hillary, Ann Gaydosh, Jerry McCann, Roger McCann, Patricia McMullen, My Benedictine Oblate family, Jack Rooney, and many others. I cannot name them all. They were all fantastic to me and I thank them sincerely.

Foreword

This book is a diary of a man full of passion and desires. The passion for Christ Jesus to be in his life, to see His love in every occurrence of his existence, both good and bad. The desire to be able to help others, may it be to people with epilepsy or those who don't. Initially, McCann wanted to help his family, to be aware about epilepsy and about Jesus, then continued on to the community through the self-help group he attends and eventually, using social media. However, this did not end here. He felt that he needed to share more, his insatiable yearning to spread awareness, help more people, drove him to write this book.

I don't see this book as just the daily journal of his sufferings, insecurities, shortcomings, deficiencies due to his health, discrimination from society, marital problems, the numerous limitations of enjoying life more. Oh no, it is not! This private diary he shares to us may cover only nine months of his life but it can definitely change our lives. This book above all else is about **compassion, courage, faith, patience, never losing hope** and about the author's greatest goal: **conversion**.

This is a must-read for people of all walks of life. Do we not feel a certain heaviness and tiredness right now in our lives? Then let the author lift you up somehow through his stories and experiences, consoling you that you are not alone; because Jesus was and is always, in our lives.

Read on and find out more surprising and intriguing facts about McCann's life….

Diary

June 15, 2011

I got up and the first thing I did today was to say a morning prayer (Divine Office). I then had breakfast and took my medication. Then I said the Lectio Divina. This is a contemplative prayer. This is reading a Bible passage and allowing the passage to speak to you. Then spend time on it. This will allow you to grow. I then went to mass. I came home to eat lunch, and I asked my wife about my brain surgery.

June 17, 2011

Last night in bed, I had a dream. I dreamed I was in high school and in a special class for slow students. I was not accepted by other students. I felt I was stupid and I was no good.

I was not allowed to take the SATs; therefore, there would not be any college. Because of my epilepsy, I was turned down by the army. I once again felt stupid. I started at a brokerage firm named Dean Witter & Company. I became an accounting clerk. Because I could not do the job right, I was fired. I then worked for the credit agency of Plainfield. Because of my epilepsy, I was fired.

I then worked at Muhlenberg Hospital. Oh, and before I worked for a credit agency in Plainfield, I worked for the South Plainfield Board of Education.

I could not sleep because I was thinking about Deanna's sickness.

June 19, 2011

I must stop this hollering; there is no reason for this. Jesus, please help me with this problem.

When I go shopping, I must be careful. There is no need for me to call Scott or create a problem. I can handle myself; I just needed to learn to be patient. Jesus, help me with this also. I must learn to stop making funny noises. I must not show my disappointment. Jesus, I pray you can help me here.

I will be going to Rome in September. I am looking forward to the trip. Epilepsy or no epilepsy, this hollering must stop. There is no reason for this. I will now say my evening prayer and listen to St. Benedict rule as an oblate. We must read one chapter each night. I also go to mass daily.

June 19, 2011

When I go shopping, I must be careful. I must go to mass now.

June 20, 2011

I must learn to stop making funny noises. Jesus, help me stop doing this.

June 22, 2011

I must learn to be patient. Jesus, help me and stay with me always. I will always trust you.

I have just died to sell. This was a great feeling.

June 23, 2011

I got up today and said my office of reading. Jesus, I want to stop this anger as I sit down and wonder what I should say next. I have just finished Lectio

Divina. This is a special prayer where you meditate and then contemplate on verses in the Bible. You read the same verse to see how it applies to you. It is very powerful that something will happen to you.

It has helped me in a lot of things. Jesus, you are always there for me. I thank you for this always.

June 25, 2011

I have just died to sell. It is a wonderful feeling, Jesus, please help me deal with the loss of a bloated mass now. I had a small seizure last night.

I lost some of my books in the computer. So now I will start my book again. We had to get a chair because the other one was broken. The time has come for us to get rides to doctors. All of us are not getting any younger.

I had another small seizure last night. I am hoping for no more seizures. Having a diary helps me to keep records of my life and also helps me to write my book. What I am is just awesome, and I'm not being funny. I no longer blame myself. Deanna is a great sport as part of my book. It is going to happen. You can bet on it. Because of my l epilepsy, I cannot help doing things in the church, and that's okay for me because I realize that this is the way to

June 28, 2011

Today I got up and said my Lectio Divina. I must pray for Deanna. She is going to see the doctors. Sadly, I cannot go to mass today because we must wait for a chair.

I must take my time in writing my book. They need to improve my attitude. They need to take responsibility for my seizures. Jesus, please help me. I'm beginning to lose my character. If this happens, I cannot help others with what they have to deal with.

Once again I must stop my hollering.

June 29, 2011

Jesus, please help me find a way to write my book. I knew you would never leave me. I will never stop trusting you. Will you help me in dealing with Deanna, with what she is going through?

June 31, 2011

Tonight I do not know why I cannot keep my cool. I tried so hard to help Deanna.

She will not let me help her. Deanna is a wonderful person if she would only tell herself so.

Jesus, I am glad you have helped me find a way to write my book.

Jesus is helping me through this mess I made. I need you near me, Jesus. I know you will not go away. If only Deanna would see herself as a wonderful person. Deanna says no one cares for her. I really try.

August 1, 2011

Jesus, what shall I do about Deanna?

August 2, 2011

Jesus, please help me with my attitude.

August 7, 2011

I had a seizure last night. What role do seizures have in my sex life? Tomorrow I must share with Dr. Oh how my sex life plays with my seizures.

I must stop making these funny noises. Jesus, I trust you will help me deal with this. I am going to Rome in September. I have never traveled alone. How do I handle this?

August 12, 2011

Today when I did my Lectio Divina, I learned about confidence in the Lord. I also learned to trust in Jesus. I can really die for my brother. I was finally able to let go of what I was holding on to for my whole life. My chat room has been a great success for epilepsy.

I am able to help others with their seizure disorder.

August 16, 2011

House: Ryanair

Today after my Lectio Divina, I read Isaiah 56:1. The Lord will stay with me no matter what happens, good or bad. Jesus, please help Deanna deal with my seizures. I must accept the fact that she is afraid of my seizures. As I write, I must deal with short-term memory which is a real hassle, but I will try very hard to get by. This I do believe. The new kit will help with my short-term memory.

I'm trying to help Deanna with the recycling. I still get very angry. I must do my best to stop this.

Deanna washes my clothes out for me every morning. I am so thankful to her for doing this.

Jesus, please help Deanna understand that there are things she can do to help me with my seizures. What started this whole thing was getting status. This was once again a big a problem.

As far as my writing, if I write, I make it legible so I can improve. People fear my seizure.

I must remember who I am, not my seizure. I must learn to accept Deanna for who she is. I continue to fail. Deanna has been through enough, and this is not being fair to her.

Deanna washes my clothes out for me every morning. I do appreciate what she does for me. I love her very, very much. She is wonderful and she is the best. It hurts Deanna to see me angry and frustrated.

I must learn not to pound on chairs. There is no need for this. Medication or no medication, there is no reason for this. I am not allowed to do this at church.

I did not feel anything about myself. I did not care about me. I could not do anything right.

I was always wrong. I thought people hated me. I was useless. I was down. My family did not care. They were embarrassed to have me around. I was never good enough for them. My brothers and sisters all went to college. But because of my epilepsy, I was not able to go. This was another reason why I put myself down. Back then, they wouldn't accept epilepsy. They thought it was taboo. Yes, I did go to a doctor, but having epilepsy was not taken seriously. Everything was against me. The whole world was against my friends (if I had any). I was just plain lost. I felt Jesus was nowhere. He was always there. I just thought He was never there. Boy, was I a mess.

All through high school, everybody stayed away from me because I had epilepsy. My seizures were very bad then. This made things worse.

What Is Epilepsy?

The brain is controlled. Neurons are tiny electrical cells that go to different parts of the brain. When the brain has too many neurons (too much electricity), this causes a seizure. Picture an orchestra. What happens when the director leaves? Then what does the orchestra do? This causes confusion. They do not know what to do, so all they do is play all the instruments at once. This is what happens when a person has a seizure. There is too much electricity in the brain.

Let's refer to epilepsy as a seizure disorder. There are about thirty different kinds of seizures. The three major types are generalized tonic-clonic (grand mal), absence (petit mal), and complex partial (psychomotor). In a generalized tonic seizure, the person will get rigid and fall to the ground. First, make sure to clear the airway. Do not restrain. Make sure his head is turned to the right so that the saliva can go out so he does not choke. The seizure will last one to three minutes. When the person comes out of the seizure, tell them they will be fine. If it lasts more than five minutes, the person will need medical assistance right away.

For complex partial seizure, the person will talk without making any sense. He will walk around and will not know where he is going. If sitting in a chair, he will pound on the arms of the chair and make it a snap his lips. Just guide him.

In an absence seizure, it the only lasts about one minute, so just be with him. So you see, there is nothing to fear. Just stay calm. There is not really too much you can do. Just be there for them.

I am not getting into this. There are several medications for seizures. There are so many things you need to do. Medications help control seizures.

My Surgery

Tests I had to have:

1. MRI (magnetic resonance imaging) is used to locate the focal point where the epilepsy is.

2. PET (positive emission tomography) is a nuclear image. There is a three-dimensional image or picture of the brain.

3. CAT's sweetness. These senior figures will go to such a nearly worthless. You reach your computerized axial tomography access in diagnosing epilepsy.

4. WADA, founded by John Wada to locate the dominant part of the brain. This OS really locates where the epilepsy is located. It is the focal point of epilepsy. This is the last test before surgery.

In my surgery, I had a left temporal lobe lumpectomy. This is the site of the brain. This is where stories were told with language memory, and it also indicates the strategies and what is practical and safe and is where parts of life are stored.

Now I'll tell you how I saw the value and was able to apply it to my life. As I look back at my family and how they felt about me, yes, it was uncomfortable for me, but as I looked at myself, I was able to grow from the experience. You see, the value was looking at myself. And most of the reasons I felt uncomfortable, I put them there myself. It was very important to see this. It is a lesson I carry with me, my entire life.

When I look at the way I was treated, the people who made fun of me, (who, I realized was making fun of me.) It was not those around me; it was me making fun of myself. Interesting, is it not? Do you see the value in being able to look at yourself? I did not see the relevance of it then, but I sure see it today.

I had many experiences of being fired, where people stayed away from me because of my epilepsy. I found all this was quite a big cop-out.

I am not saying I was not hurt, but I was using that hurt to feel sorry for myself. I was playing pity. The value in this is acceptance, that I was able to see myself in this way.

At one time I wanted to become a deacon in the Catholic Church. Everyone in my family supported me very well. My wife, Deanna, was a major part in supporting me in this venture. No one could talk to me and tell me that it would not work.

I was too blind to see it would not work. There were doctors and lawyers, people with college degrees, and I was not one of them. Down here is where I really looked at myself and saw the value.

I value that I was able to look at myself very, very hard and saw that this was not who I was and that it was okay. This was a part of life where I was able to see, that who I am was not to destroy people's lives, especially those

I love. I learned a very valuable lesson. Having Jesus with me, made me see this experience does not work.

Okay, now and today, with the help of Jesus, I can stop these angry feelings I get when something goes wrong. With the help of Jesus, I can stop this hollering.

I just wish I can stop making the weird noises I do not need to make. Please Jesus, help.

I went to my neurologist today. I had a very good report. I just had small seizures. With the help of Jesus through my prayers, I am able to do this. There is so much value to life. As long as we are responsible and really know ourselves and love ourselves, we can move mountains. We are all wonderful people, and we really do care and we really do matter no matter what happens to us. Good, bad, or indifferent, there is value in everything. If we look hard enough, we will always find the value.

You will also find that if you care about the people who surround you, you will see how wonderful they are. Then they will love you no matter what is said by you or them. Love is always there.

January 19, 2012

I just had a seizure now and it made me quite tired. I was not too happy. Besides being tired, makes me very angry. I asked Jesus how I should handle this. Jesus allowed me to accept myself for who I am and that it was okay. I told Him that it does not help my wife, Deanna. So I can see now that with Jesus's help, I can allow myself to grow. So you see, even in the present day, if you allow it, you can become a better person. Jesus let me realize how wonderful life is. I was really able to see that no matter what happens or how I feel about it, I can always make it work. It makes me feel better about what happens each day. It helps me realize the importance of helping other people who are worse off than me. I also must find a way. Medication or not, I must find a way to stop my temper and making these funny noises. I do not need to jump up every time something happens to me. I must learn to keep an appropriate way of acting. So you see, even in the present day, the problems I have never ceased. I feel very bad that I cannot help my wife, Deanna, with all the doctors' appointments she needs to go to. I cannot drive, so it makes me feel very bad. I really wish I could help somehow.

I am now going to say the evening prayer.

January 31, 2012

Today, I finally got my Dragon to work. I had a terrible time. Over and over I tried to get it to work. I must learn to stop getting so upset when something happens to me. There is no need for me to sound off. Jesus, please help me to act accordingly. I need to calm down, especially when talking to Deanna. I must learn to always stay calm. Jesus, please help me with all the problems that I am having. Today I was getting upset over nothing. I need a lot of help. I need to be kind and treat Deanna the way she should be treated.

So I am now able to continue with my book. I still need to know that my book will work. I need a lot of prayers, coverage, and insight above all others. I must remain to have a good attitude always. With Jesus, I will get what I need. He will never leave me. I will always need prayer in my life.

Today, there was no need for me to act the way I did. These I must do. See, it was my lack of patience that caused me not to understand if I was doing things right. What happened today would not have happened if I stayed with a cool head. If you noticed today I was very repetitious. This is because of my surgery. When I had the brain surgery, the surgeon cut the part where the short memory was located. This is why parts of the book are very repetitious.

February 1, 2012

So far today things are good. I'm still making those funny noises every time something happens. Somehow I need to stop with this. There is no need for making these noises.

I also must be careful and look at what I am doing. Yes, I know the medication makes me unsteady on my feet, but because of this, I must be careful and look at where I'm going. If I do, this things can and will be better with the help of Jesus and strong prayer, and knowing that Jesus will never leave me is an awesome feeling. Today I had to make a new seizure record for starting on February 1, 2012. The last few days and nights, my left leg has been very weak. And because of this, all my left shoulder hurts me when I go to bed and who it.

I pray the Divine Office today. I also said Lectio Divina. This type of prayer is a slow meditation. You allow yourself to a verse of the Bible and allow the verse of the Bible to see how your life is, by meditating on the verse and immersing yourself in it. Read the verse about five times, and you will see that each time you read the verse, the stronger your meditation becomes. The last time you read, you will be able to see how it applies to your life. When I finish meditating, what I have read from the Bible becomes a real part of my life. As I read the Bible daily, I really find that Jesus is with me and never leaves me. I will now say my daytime prayer and then go rest.

February 2, 2012

I would like to share today what I learned about Deanna. It would be much easier for her if she would only allow herself to go easier on herself. She does nothing but put herself down. She says things and always blames herself. What has happened? I wish she would realize that she is a wonderful person with very good qualities. If she would only realize this herself. I love her very much. I must remember that I am part of all of this because of the way I holler. Jesus, I must find a way to stop her from becoming uncomfortable with me. When I like the new shoes I put on, there is no reason for me to holler and make funny noises.

Jesus, what causes these funny noises? Is it the medication? Could this be a side-effect? Jesus, is this just a challenge that you have given me? If so, allow me to realize that it is.

I am having some trouble with my balance. Please help me. Jesus, one thing I fear is losing my attitude. It happens. I am sunk. I just sent part of this book I have and trust that I will get insight that I need. Jesus, was this the right thing to do? Jesus, you are always there. I realized this when I gave my Lectio Divina and my Divine Office. These two prayers are very strong and stayed with me throughout the day. Again, what is bothering me today is whether or not this book will work. I am going to mass today. It is the Feast of the Presentation of our Lord. This feast is where the child Jesus is presented by Mary in the temple. This is also the feast where candles are lit. Before I continue, I will find out why candles are used.

Tomorrow is the feast of St. Blaise, where your throat is blessed. I shall find out the meaning of this feast after mass today. I am now going to get ready for mass, so I put on my coat.

When I came in from mass, I sat down to watch television and it would not go on, so I started to swear. There is no need for this, seeing that every time I open my mouth, there is nothing but inappropriate language. Jesus, please help me with this. I somehow need to stop. I am having a terrible time in trying to stop this. I do not know what to do. I need to pray for this. My wife does not need to be exposed to this. Jesus, please show me the way to work on this. I really need to stop this. Jesus, I know you're with me and will never leave me. You will never leave me. I really do feel your presence and also the presence of the Holy Spirit. Jesus I do not mean to be so repetitious, but I really need your help with this problem. It does not seem to stop no matter what I do. I know I still have in me such a wonderful attitude. If this is so, where is this filthy mouth from? Jesus, please help my wife, Deanna, with this mess she is now going through. For her, it is not pleasant.

On another issue, we are never going to move. This is a big challenge for me. Jesus, I know you will be with me and help me accept this challenge.

Please help me see my wife, Deanna, for who she is, as a wonderful person. I love her very, very much. Only Deanna has been and is always with me through all my accidents.

The first accident was when I was in a cafeteria. I fell off a ladder and broke both of my arms. Accident number two, I had a bad mishap with my car. I totally messed it up, and then another car. After this, my driving has become a real burden to Deanna. I messed up not only my life, but I also messed hers up.

There was also this matter wherein at one time I wanted to become a deacon diocese of Metuchen, New Jersey. I was the only one who was not aware that it would not work. My wife, Deanna, my family, and all my friends did not want to hurt my feelings, so they signed all the papers for me to become a deacon. Meanwhile, I found out that there were doctors, lawyers and, teachers, who would certainly fit the profile.

You see, this is where you learn lessons. As I look back at this, I see the significance of that incident. I learned that you cannot be who you're not. In whatever you do, always be who you are and not something you're not. Yes, the experience was not pleasant, but it's one thing to be able to see the value of all this, and it makes me a better person.

If you look at what I have written with each passing day, each experience was bad or indifferent. There is great value in just being you. If you allow this, you can move mountains.

As I look back to what I have written, I can see it is so repetitious. I can see where my short-term memory plays a big part and will continue to be, for this book. It makes me wonder if this will ever work.

February 2, 2012

Today is the feast of St. Blaise, who blesses your throat. This is a Catholic tradition. St. Blaise takes care of your health. His expertise is your throat.

I also am still making those funny noises today. Jesus, I still need help with this problem. Why doesn't it seem to stop? You know, Jesus, I am still carrying on with this problem. There is no need for all of this. I must find a way for this to be stopped. Today I prayed my Lectio Divina. This type of prayer is when we contemplate with the scripture five times. Each time you allow yourself to listen attentively and slowly and each time to see the growth within yourself, and if you pray slowly, you will realize your growth. This morning when I got up, I prayed my Divine Office and grew even more. Prayer is very, very strong. This morning I was able to put my walking shoes on correctly. Point out hollering. But I still need to work on this. I have a great attitude but I need to find some way to stop this hollering and getting excited. I need to slow down. I need to find some way to relax. Now, if I can only learn to do this and see the significance of it, I will become a much better person with each day. I can look at my experiences and grow and become a better person. Jesus, I need to be able to understand Deanna and allow her to be who she is, and that is she must remember that she is a wonderful person. I need your help in allowing her to see this. When I sent part of the book out to all my friends and family, I trust they will not get offended by so many things I said while growing up. Especially regarding the notions I had that, I thought they did not care about me, that I was not good enough. I wanted them to see that although I had a negative experience with them, I hope for them to see my life and that they were a big part of my growing up.

Again I realize it now if you allow yourself to be who you are and not someone else, then you grow. You will have growth and vitality. You will have compassion arising. That's the right path to follow Jesus. Look at the reward we get from being with Jesus. The above is what I got out of my contemplative prayer, and in so doing, I really became a better person this time. It is because of Jesus, and it is not of my own doing.

February 3, 2012

I can see why in writing this book, I grow each day. If this will never sell, it is great therapy. I'm able to realize many things I never saw before. When I do good or bad, there is value in everything if I allow it.

Jesus, please help me with my seizures. I have them about once a month. My goal is to never have another seizure, even a small one. Jesus, please show me how this could be. Will I ever be able to make this happen? Remind me when I go see Dr. Geller. I can look forward to never having a seizure again. Fortunately, I continue to take my medication in the right manner. Oh, I even noticed today that when I was in the bathroom, something was not going right, so I grabbed the paper towel rack and shook on it because I was angry, and once again I made a funny noise. This is where I need to calm down. This is where I need to conquer this. I need to have patience. Why is it that I consistently do this? This is where my character needs to change. Jesus, is this part of my character? And is this really right? Or is it something I should recognize that will never change?

Jesus please show me this can still be changed. I need to become much more patient in everything I do, especially becoming calm. If I can achieve this, I will become a better person no matter what. One thing I must do is not let it go to my head. Big heads do not work in my life. All you need to do is remember who you are as a person. Remember who we are, we are awesome people and wonderful people. We must love ourselves and know that we do count. We do matter no matter what. Whatever happened to us does not define us. Remember we do count. It always always matters. I cannot stress that enough.

February 4, 2012

I must also recognize we will never, never move. I think the reason is that my wife, Deanna, wants to see her son Joseph alive. I must recognize that this is part of who she is and will never change. If only she would put this in the right perspective, she would make the problem much easier on herself. She blames everything on herself; everything is always all her fault. She is not being very fair to herself. She is a wonderful person. I only wish she would recognize this. She does so much for everybody, and she does not get some credit for this. It is not always all her fault. As far as I am concerned, I need to stop all this mess. I always make her very, very angry. Yes, I do holler at her very much. There is no reason for me to do this. I must look at this and see how much I can change. I am sure that if I face this, I'll be able to perceive the value in the progress I have made. But it was hard to see a change from what the situation looks like. This could help our entire relationship. We do care for each other, we just don't see it.

I know that Jesus is with me, and He will never leave me. He will always get me through this mess I made. As long as I never lose my faith and my prayer, I will always have compassion and love for the people I care for and the people I love. I will always be able to see Jesus in me. He is also in each one of us. If we can just be with one another, you all can care, have compassion, and pray for one another. We would often move mountains and whatever else is in our path.

Today I got up at seven in the morning for the office. My Lectio Divina, as I have stated before, is a prayer in which you contemplate and read a scripture from the Bible five times. Each time you apply it to your life. At about ten thirty this morning, Deanna and I went to South Plainfield to look for a night table. We found one that Deanna liked very much, however when we reached home, the table broke down. And that made Deanna very sad. My friend Scott came over and took us to a few furniture stores where we could find a nightstand that worked, but Deanna was still unhappy. I wish Deanna would realize that she is getting herself agitated on a stupid night table. She is a wonderful person.

If only she would not make herself so wrong and give herself some credit for everything that she does. I realized that no matter what I do I cannot help her when she herself is still not happy with the situation. Jesus, please help me with this mess. I am maintaining my faith. Jesus, am I doing wrong by trying to help? Isn't this helping? Or am I making things worse? I need faith so I can be strong. This problem is now in Your hands. Give me some direction as to what I should do.

February 5, 2012

Today is Sunday, the fourth week in ordinary time. Here is the gospel of Mark 1:29–39:

I'm leaving the synagogue. Jesus entered the house of Simon and Andrew, along with James, and John. Simon's mother-in-law is very sick with a fever. They immediately told him about her as He approached then grabbed her by the hand and helped her up. Then Jesus left. And she waited on them until it was evening. After sunset, people brought to Him all who are ill or possessed by demons. The whole town was gathering at the door. He cured many who were sick with various diseases, and He drove out many demons, not permitting them to speak because they knew Him.

Rising very early before dawn, He left and went off to a deserted place, where He prayed. Simon and those who were with Him, finding Him, said, "Everyone is looking for you." He told them, "Let us go on to nearby villages that I may preach there also. For this purpose, I have come." So He went into the synagogues, preaching and driving out demons from the whole of Galilee.

I would like to share what I got out of this gospel. Jesus preaches with authority, not as we look at authority, but to look in their eyes and allow them to see who they are as people, to look into their hearts.

I need to share what just came out for me today. It is the wisdom I have gained by reading scriptures. Isn't it strange how the gospel of Mark got me? I am now talking about wisdom. To be who you are does not mean you need to be a professor, a teacher, a doctor, or a lawyer or someone that is more informed and more knowledgeable. We can be ourselves because, with Jesus and your faith in Him, you know that Jesus will never leave you.

When the tax man called today, there was no reason for her to be upset. She should not have allowed herself to be mistreated. Jesus, please allow me to see and be with her. She is not being herself.

Here is 1 Corinthians 9:16–19; 22–23. Brothers and sisters, for if I preach the gospel. There is no reason for me to boast about this obligation has been entrusted to me, and woe to me if I do not preach it! If I do so willingly, I have recompense, but if I do it unwillingly there, I am entrusted with a stewardship. What then is my recompense? I offered the gospel free of charge so as not to make full use of my right in the gospel.

Although I am free from everyone's expectations, I have made myself a servant to all of them to win more people. To the weak, I became weak in order to win the weak. I have become all things to all people so that by all possible means I might save some of them. I do all this for the sake of the gospel in order to have a share in its blessing.

Job 7:1–7

Joel spoke, saying, "Is not man's life on earth a drudgery? Are not his days those of harming? Is a slave who longs for the shape a heart a highly who waits for his wages. So I have been assigned most of it; misery and troubled nights have been allotted to me. If I didn't say, "When shall I arise now?" And the night drags on. I am filled with restlessness until dawn. My days are swifter than a weaver's shuttle may come to him and out went hope.

Remember that my life is like the wind; I shall not see happiness again.

So you see if you read this scripture, we can allow ourselves to be happy even when troubles are around. If we believe the scripture of Job, you can see that Job was very unhappy. However, Job learned to turn this unhappiness into being happy. This is how you contemplate so that the scripture applies to us. I really see today's readings are very powerful. You read the Bible every day, a different Scripture every day, and if you contemplate on one slowly, you can see its power. Today has been a very strong day of prayer for me. This is where Jesus never loses me. I always have direction. As long as I have great faith and strong prayer life, I have nothing to fear. I will now go and say my evening prayer.

February 6, 2012

As I said my morning prayer this morning, I felt the great strength in my prayer. It is beginning to allow me to see Deanna the way she is. I just wish she would accept herself in the same manner. If she will only care for herself, she would see how beneficial it would be. However, I must adjust and allow myself to understand that this will not change. Jesus, this is where you come in. Please guide me as to what I should do. She is very upset today because the tax man keeps changing appointments for doing the income tax. This makes her very upset. Jesus, should I go to our internist Dr. Sedick? I think I should go to the bone doctor regarding my left leg. However, I think I am making Deanna wrong. I think I am only having hard feelings. Jesus, do you think this is true?

Following is the role my wife, Deanna, helped with on our trip to Baltimore:

> I am writing this all down for you because I am afraid I will not remember everything. When I bring my husband to your office. You know, he had seizures when we went to Baltimore on a bus trip on Saturday, September 28, 2010. The first one came on so suddenly as we left the restaurant. He stopped and then said gibberish and that type of talking and ran. I caught up with him, just about pulled him for blocks, until we came back to our bus to the pickup area. I saw a man from the trip and asked for his help, and he watched me and helped me to get him on the bus. Jean was totally unresponsive for about fifty minutes. Just sitting on the bus bench and not talking or doing anything. When the bus pulled up the man who helped Jean get on the bus got off and he suddenly looked around to see all was fine. About four o'clock, the bus took us to our hotel, and we went to our room to unpack and freshen up and almost missed the five o'clock bus that was coming to take us back in town for dinner and then to the Yankee game. Everything was fine until we went to wait for the bus and then my husband

began to talk gibberish again. I told the bus driver to leave since he could not travel at this time after almost an hour his seizure wind down. We then took the Metro to the ballpark, and everything was fine. Next, we were left all at the harbor, and we ate and stopped as everyone else did after a while. He wants to know why we didn't do any touring. He did not remember, the day before the tour, I said I would dissuade him to the contrary! The trip was soon coming to a close, and our bus came at four o'clock to bring us home. He had a couple small seizures after church on Sunday, October 28. Just gibberish and waving hands. On Monday, November 4, he had a small seizure around six o'clock. In talking I found him just in waving his hands again; he was fine. He rode his bike about ten times after I spoke with you, claiming he did not remember you saying he could not write. Maybe the whole weather has stopped him on this.

He so wants to travel, but I do not like him flying wherever he wants all by himself. There is no guarantee that he would be seizure-free. And I don't believe, whoever he'll be staying with would want the responsibility of a senior guard while he is visiting. A year ago, he went against our plea and traveled, he'd had seizures. His very well-educated older brother panicked and called Dr. Siddiq on what to do. He is married and has two-year-old children. It's all good when they are all together having fun and games, but what then when the children are in school? There would be no one with him. I cannot take all the work at the drop of a hat. I must have this job and the money. I need to take into consideration my pension and also my self-esteem. What can be done? Oh, here is something I copied from the recent CPR at work: while these symptoms are not frequent, they could still mean harm.

As much as I care about my wife and my brother, there is much education about seizure disorders that are not out there. People need to know that they do not have to panic if they are well-informed about seizures. It is unfortunate that my wife, Deanna, refuses to learn the procedure when a seizure occurs. I have previously explained to her what to do when someone has a seizure. There is no need to get upset if you know what to do. The shame is I have tried to explain it, but they do not accept this. Jesus, this is where you come in. Please advise me as to what I should do since they will not let me explain.

February 7, 2012

As I said my morning prayers and Lectio Divina. I learned that even when great patience and wisdom are given to me to care for others. If I do not care for Jesus, I will still find myself loving money and material things. This is why we cannot love God and love worldly things at the same time. If you love Jesus, be kind to others, love the people around you and the people that are close to you. Because when you make them happy, this brings happiness to yourself too. Jesus, I have great faith in you. I need to stop this hollering and losing patience. There is no need for this, and thus, please give me the strength to stop all this. Please help me. Somehow, I need to stop this. I will continue praying. I can pray in the office, and I will continue praying about this. I know you will help me.

I must continue to help my wife, Deanna, with what she is going through. I told her yesterday that she should not let people walk on her or be mean to her. But she said that she is already doing what she thinks is right. So, Jesus, how should I handle this? I love her very much. I want so much to allow herself to be who she is. Jesus, is this possible for me to do this?

Here is a change of subject. I am now watching a parade for the football team the Giants in the Super Bowl, and they are now celebrating in New York. They are having a ticker tape parade down the Canyon of Heroes in New York City. The mayor of New York will give them the keys to New York.

Now I want to get back on track. I just sent my spiritual director an e-mail to say hello. Perhaps we can meet to have our monthly meeting. I would say that Mary Joe has been a huge part of my life; she has helped me through the years. My spiritual direction helps me in my life very much. As to knowing who I am. It was just yesterday when I wrote what Deanna said about our trip to Baltimore. I had many seizures. Despite her refusal to learn what to do when I have a seizure, she was there with me. I am now going to do mass. Father George spoke today about growing up when we were children. He explained that as children, we do not know much about our faith, but we do grow up. We get to realize that we recognize more about our faith. We never stop learning and it just keeps getting stronger. I am now going to say my daytime prayer.

After reading my contemplative prayer today, I realized that trusting in the Lord works very well in my life

The gospel of Mark 7:1–13:

When the Pharisees with some of the scribes had come from Jerusalem gathered around Jesus, they observed that some of His disciples ate their meals with unclean hands, that is, unwashed—hands. For the Pharisees and all the Jews do not eat unless they carefully washed their hands, keeping the tradition of the elders. Anything coming from the marketplace, they do not eat without dipping them in waters. And there were many other things that they have additionally observed—the purification of cups and jugs and kettles—and so the Pharisees and the scribes questioned him. Why don't your disciples follow tradition and instead ate their meals with unclean hands? He responded well. Isaiah's prophecy about you hypocrites is written. These people honor me with their lips, but their hearts are far from me. In vain do they worship me, teaching doctrines with human precepts?

In this regard, God's commandment is that but cling to human tradition. He went on to say, "How well you have set aside the commandment of God in order to hold your tradition." When Moses said, "Honor your father and mother," any support you might have had for the qorban meeting is dedicated to God. You allow him to do nothing more with his father and mother. "You no longer honor the word of God, in favor of your traditions that you have handed down. You do many such things."

So you see, by honoring your mother and your father, in reading this gospel, we can see how we were brought up as children into respecting others. When we respect others we respect ourselves. We learn to love each other and ourselves. It is really a nice feeling to be able to see this and in being able to express this.

February 8, 2012

I watched a television program last night. It was all about whether I had done this or that. And what would have happened if you have done that?

What if I do not have epilepsy? What if I did go to college? What if I did become a monk or a priest? What if I joined the army? What if I was not fired from my jobs so much? What if I did not get divorced? What if I did not live the gay style of life for a period of time in my life? What would have happened if I did not get married? What would my life be like?

Okay, the above I have learned is nothing but a big pity party, which I found in life does not work. Who I am is not all these things. These things I have done they all may be true, but who I am is who I am. This was a big part of my life, and it was all true, but I have grown from the experience. So you see, the important thing is growing.

This is where my prayer comes in. And Jesus never leaves me. Because You never left me, I am not the one who caused this. It is my faith in Jesus. I pray to always maintain the strong faith that I have.

Once again, Jesus, I am still carrying on with the hollering, making noises, writing on things like lack of patience. Jesus, I really somehow must find a way to control these. There was no need for this to happen. Jesus, show me a way that I can stop all this. I do need to stop. I am now going to eat my lunch. Okay, here's more. What if I did not wreck cars? What if my family standards were like everybody else's, and I was not disabled (was not in hospitals so much). Maybe my wife, Deanna, would have no fear of me because of epilepsy. When she did choose to understand, the others around me chose to understand my epilepsy.

My point is this never happened because it never happened. I cannot do anything. I cannot change anything. It happens and cannot be undone. The only thing is the growth from the experience. So you can see, in life, no matter what happens to you, good or bad, there is great value in all of them, but we must learn to grow from these experiences

February 9, 2012

I got up this morning and said my morning prayer. I learned about forgiveness and how we should forgive others. If we forgive our friends, we are able to forgive ourselves.

My wife, Deanna, is a wonderful person. She washed my shirt and pants and made me breakfast. Now once again I am starting to get angry. I am getting aggravated—pounding my hands. I'm getting too excited. I'm beginning to have no patience. Jesus, please help me not to do this. I know that this is not right, and it upsets everyone around me, especially my beautiful wife, Deanna. She is always so wonderful. She always bears with me in my time of need. If I was only patient, I would understand what is going on with my constantly getting upset.

Deanna knows that the chair in the living room was damaged. I got very upset that we could not find the paperwork. She and I looked all over the place and could not find it. We looked through all my files and still did not find it there. I finally realized that no matter what was said, what was done was not going getting our chair fixed. So we went from store to store. I was very proud of Deanna. She says she is afraid of people. However, she handled this problem with the chair like a trooper. The issue with the chair was handled in about five minutes. She should be very, very proud of herself. She can do things that she needs to do. They will be coming March 1 to fix the chair.

Jesus, please help me with my attitude. I was just thinking that if I could drive, none of this would happen. My point again is all that has happened to me, already happened to me, I cannot turn back the clock. I can only go on and grow to become a better person. These kinds of things I get to look at. I am not happy with them and they need to change. So you see, the value here is in improving my life and become a better person. Another problem that I have is when working on the computer. I get too excited. If I did not get this way, I would not have so much lack of patience. It is not the computer; it's me. I must work on myself to improve the way I act and the way I talk.

On another note, I played another pity party. I thought Mary Jo, my spiritual director, should have called me. I felt very unhappy because she did not answer my e-mails. I felt she did not care about me. This was once again the acting out, feeling sorry for myself. The value I saw in this was that the pity parties do not fit in my life.

I must ask Scott to help me take the table back the store where Deanna bought it. She is getting very, very angry that the table is not gone yet.

February 10, 2012

Today I was just thinking about keeping my sanity regarding the house. I would like to move out of the house because neither one of us is getting younger. We do not need the headaches of owning a big house with tenants. All we need is something small just for us. But for some reason, she will not. I believe that the house was on the market. The house was more than likely to be sold. I do wish we would sell the house. But it will not happen. It's just like she does not want to give up this house. But she refuses to make this easy for her. I must somehow accept that moving out of here is not going to happen.

Scott and I are going to bring the table back. The table was broken and needs to go back to the store, so Scott and I will bring it back to South Plainfield where it was bought. This should make her happy. I am now going to rest after I say my daytime prayer.

February 10, 2012

I am just thinking now that my life is very boring. Most of the days, I really do the same thing, because if I do not drive, it makes me feel useless to everyone. I do not feel I can be of any value to anyone. I need somehow to find a way to read newspapers, books, and other materials that benefit me. Jesus, I need your help to help me feel that I do contribute, that I may realize things are the way they are because that's the way are. But with your help, I can change all this. Please find a way to give me some energy so I can contribute, not to make me feel useless.

As you can see, we never stop the pity parties. What I am really feeling sorry for is myself. The only way I can grow out of this is to realize this is part of life, that it does happen and that you are not wrong. What happened made you a wonderful person. And these pity parties never work. This is your responsibility. What just happened is OK, but you can grow from this. You do not have to react in a negative way every time something is said to you. For example, when Deanna talks to you, you should react in a way that works for both of you. Always keep cool and answer appropriately. This will make all feel better. Deanna needs to be reassured that people do care about her and that a lot of times they have their own life. Now I'm supposed to go to St. Mary's Abbey in Morristown to have our monthly oblate meeting. It is possible that they may not have a meeting. It is also possible I may not be able to get there.

I am now going to say my evening prayer.

February 11, 2012

I just fell out of my computer chair and I am up to my old tricks. Started hollering again, swerving again, and getting upset. Once again, there's no need for this. Somehow all of this needs to stop. There is not the easy way. There is no need for this. Jesus, please help me find a way that I may act appropriately regarding all of these. I truly need your help. I blame no one else but me; it was truly my fault.

After reading my Lectio (well, you read a verse from the Bible), I contemplated slowly on each verse. This allows you to discover what is going on in your life. You read each verse about five times. Each time you allow yourself to grow. One verse was about caring for others; the next was about compassion for others. It may be realized that if you have these qualities, you will be able to help others. In so doing, become a much better person and learn from it.

In the Bible, others stayed away from people who have leprosy because this was contagious. It was a real shame. Today, in my case, it was my epilepsy. People stayed away from me. It was not pleasant. When I allow myself and accept myself for what I was and who I was, I am able to help others who are much worse than I am. This is where Jesus helps with your compassion and also with your caring.

I am just thinking now that because I am not driving, I might not be able to get around. People do not care about me, and I am not much use to anyone.

I am playing another pity party. What you learn from all these bad things that happen to you, you can use all of this to make you grow as a person, a better person. You must remember that you're a wonderful person; it always counts and matters. So you see, every day that goes by, there is great value in it. Life is so beautiful. Maintaining this attitude matters. One thing that Jesus helps you with, are these qualities; your compassion and caring. Sharing what I did today helps my character no matter what. My fear is that I may lose this. But with my faith in Jesus, I will not lose it.

February 11, 2012

Things are not working today. Deanna says everybody is making fun of her. She does nothing right, and she makes all these mistakes, and everything is always her fault, and once again Deanna blames herself. There is no way she should be blaming herself for any of this. Deanna is wonderful to me. She put out my clothes; she makes the breakfasts.

If Deanna would only look inside herself, she will realize she's a wonderful person and a caring person. If Deanna would only realize the fact that she is amazing and people love her no matter what, things could be different.

I would like to sell this house. If Deanna would only realize that this would be a very good move. She and I are not getting any younger. We do not need this large home. We do not need the responsibility of having to take care of this home. All we need is something small. Just something for us. I wish Deanna would realize this. It could have been much, much different for both of us. This is where my strong faith and prayer comes in. This is where our Lord Jesus comes in.

Let's change the subject: I am a disabled person, falling is not my fault. It's these floors. They jump out at me. When I sit in chairs, they will move.

This is the reason I have a cane is to hold the floor down. You need to make fun of yourself. You need to laugh at these things to keep your sanity. I am not saying that they are not serious, but let's have some fun. This is where you turned serious things that happened, to make you grow as a person, a better and happy person. So you see, with every experience you have, you are able to look at yourself and use all the experiences and grow from them.

February 12, 2012

I have learned today from going to mass about caring for others who are less fortunate, by being compassionate, by forgiving others. When I did Lectio Divina, a verse from the Bible under the will of Moses, there was a leper who was unclean, and because his being unclean, the leper had to live alone until he was cured by a miracle. He could go back to a normal life in the community. Next, in 1 Corinthians, Paul tells us to do all things with the glory of God and offer it up. So you see, the disease might be unpleasant to look at, but we can grow from it. In Mark's gospel, Jesus cures a leper with the touch of His hand so that men can rejoin the community again. So let's look at our own lives and see where the pain may be. In my case, it was my epilepsy. People stay away from me; however, once I took responsibility for what I have, I was able to recognize I have a great gift,

Jesus, and to be able to help others who are worse off than I was. It is a great reward to be able to do this. Because of strong prayer, because of my faith, I am able to live a beautiful life.

My wife has shared with me something I can learn and apply to my life. Deanna had talked about education. It seems that her girlfriend was getting married. Apparently, formal education counts more than being a truck driver, since Mary Lou was a nurse and Ed, her husband-to-be was a truck driver, it was thought that the marriage would not work; However, they have been married forty-eight years. Now tell me, doesn't that count? What has been stated regarding marriage is really no one's fault, but people will always be like this. We should never judge people and should allow them to be who they are and that is the way it should be for them. What other people think is not important. You must realize that that does not work, and life is not all about getting a good or formal education, but it is the compassion and love you have for others.

Another thing that just occurred to me is the fact that I am an oblate of St. Benedict, a group of people with a strong relationship with God by praying with St. Benedict. 73 rules.

February 12, 2012

Let me read St. Benedict's rule 47: Signaling Times for the Work of God

The superior responsibility is for making sure that time was the work of God, both at night and during the day. It is clearly made known to all, this way of course, by delegating the responsible members of the community pool and the reliant to make sure that everything is done at the proper time.

The superior is followed by other authorized members of the community. They had to be in order. You aim the light, singing songs and antiphons and psalms for the choir. One of those, however, should come forward to seeing and being who has the ability to fulfill this role in a way that is helpful to others, and all must play their part of the directions of the superior and humility and strength out one of relevance to God.

This is one rule that is the issue of obedience. As you can see, this will applies to our lives and teaches us to obey what Jesus tells us to.

Now, Jesus, I am still making those weird noises when I am ready to fall. I still have a great lack of patience. Now I can have a great attitude. I can be myself, and I am a wonderful person.

If this is true, then where is all this garbage coming from?

On another note, why does my wife, Deanna, choose to combine? Could it be that the fact that I cannot provide is because of the fact that I cannot drive? I am not able to hear her out. Jesus, how do I handle this? I do feel very bad about this, that I cannot provide her transportation.

You know, I was just thinking that I can still use whatever is said about me, how I feel about me, how I feel about what people say about me, only I feel about what they say and how strongly I feel and felt myself. At times I do write that about myself, about the usefulness and about how no one cares that I even exist now from this. I feel so, so sorry for myself. My, what a pity party. Let me go on with my life and stop. Look at this. There is great value in looking at what just happened to me. Things can be so negative, and when you get out of this negativity after it is all done, you never stop growing into a much better person. I must pursue the fact that no matter what, everyone has wonderful qualities, and let's allow them to bring joy to all. There is so much we can give one another. If we would only allow everyone to be who they are. Well, that is all I can think of for today. I will now say my daytime prayer.

If I should think of anything else, I shall come back and continue my diary. Peace and God bless.

February 13, 2012

Okay, I lost my cell phone. I am once again starting to make those funny noises, and my big mouth is acting up and I'm swearing. Jesus, this is what I'm trying to stop. I'm also making foolish statements. I am also telling my wife, Deanna, that I am going to cease to exist. This is not the appropriate thing to say. So, Jesus, I must stop this foolishness. There is no need for me to carry on like this. Please once again help me. Please help my wife, Deanna, to attend to her troubles; I do not want to add more to them. Jesus, I know this will work out.

I am now going to tell the people I meet and care about what to do when I have a seizure, but I only think it's fair this way; they will have no cause to fear me. They will know exactly what to do if a seizure occurs. It is only fair that I do this. I do believe this.

My sister Eileen sent me an e-mail last night that really picked up my spirits. She thanked me for sharing part of my book and told me that I have great faith in God. She also said that I should never give up because my God is there throughout my life. Well, I had better get ready for church. Please give me the strength to share with the people I care about regarding my seizures.

Today, when I said my contemplative prayer, I learned all about forgiveness and the Jewish people not liking tax collectors because of their cheating and greediness by keeping the extra money for themselves. They also could not understand how Jesus can cure because only God can cure. They did not understand. God forgave the paralytic. He forgave his sins first and then his body. This shows that all sins can be forgiven. The best lesson we can learn is to forgive others. By forgiving others, we forgive ourselves. This is how we grow as a person and become a better person. If you allow yourself to do this then you can. It is the greatest feeling. Jesus is showing me a way to help my wife, Deanna, to allow her to see who she really is and how wonderful she is.

Oh, I am thinking about moving to a new house. Neither one of us is getting any younger. We do not need this big house nor the responsibility that comes with it. All we need is something for ourselves. Jesus, it is not the case of money. We are not rich but we are not poor either. Please help me help Deanna understand this. In my case, I think I would have fewer seizures or then perhaps no seizure at all. Jesus, I still need your help in making me stop the constant hollering, funny noises, and being more careful in watching out when I walk. I know I have trouble walking, but I can also be careful and watch what I am doing. Jesus, once again I need your help in acting appropriately. With my faith and strong prayer, I can make this happen. I know you will never leave me. You are and always with me.

It has just been brought to my attention by Deanna that I continue to keep on falling constantly. They found a cut on my leg. The cut came from when I fell on the side of the bed. It was the bed frame; I think I scraped my leg from the side of the bed. That is the only thing that I can think of. At least now I am able to admit that I am falling, as I would deny before. The men were just here putting a transformer on the furnace. I am now finding it very hard to walk. My left leg is getting worse.

I haven't been able to tell people what to do when a seizure comes. Jesus, please give me the strength to continue to do this. We received some income tax forms. Some of them need to be signed and sent back to Bob S., and there is a form for income tax we must keep for next year. Deanna has just called me regarding the plumber fixing the furnace. He bought a new transformer. It was much cheaper than the company we dealt with. The main game is his personal card, to call him when something else happens regarding the furnace. I thought that was very good that he did that. I just got a little excited because I had lost some of the documents for my new book. It turns out that no documents were lost. Gene, let's not get too excited. So, slow down.

Gene, nothing has happened.

Because of my seizures, Deanna has a great fear of me in bed. While having sex, I will hurt her. But I do love her. She is afraid, you see, many years ago, I had a generalized tonic-clonic seizure where I did her during sex and she will never forget that. I must be able to feel the satisfaction when I'm having sex with her. I would like it to be known that I am not trying to be facetious. I am just sharing the way I feel regarding having sex with her. Deanna is still a wonderful person and a caring person. This is the part that I do love of Deanna.

I have not had a seizure this year yet. It is now the middle of February 2012. So let's see if we can make it until March. I think that as long as I take my medication, I can make it until March 2012. I can make it with the help of Jesus. I will now go rest after saying my daytime prayer.

Peace and God bless.

I just got up from resting and finishing my evening prayer. Deanna just came back from Ann's, her friend. She gave us some Charlie Brown coupons. Charlie Brown is a type of restaurant. Deanna also went across the street, getting the bill for our landscaping. I do believe she received the income tax papers. I must not forget to write a check for the PAL league. I believe I gave them a check for $500. I must try to start reading newspapers, also books. I need to become informed about the news and happenings around me. I was very successful in sharing with people what they should do if I have a seizure.

They are no longer afraid and they know what to do in case I have a seizure. Deanna does not have to prepare for me. It is wonderful what she does when she is not required to do it, but I guess she knows no other way. This is all a part of who Deanna is. I will always love her. I have flowers coming for Deanna. She says she does not want them, but I think she does.

Happy Valentine's Day, Deanna. I love you. You are wonderful. You are a special individual. At times I have done nothing but cause you trouble, but you will always be wonderful in my eyes.

Deanna, I am going to be a better person.

I got up this morning. It got washed and dressed. Today is Valentine's Day. Deanna and the cats gave me some socks for Valentine's Day. Deanna will be surprised when she receives flowers delivered to her today. She will not expect them. I am giving them to her because I love her.

I learned today that the Holy Spirit is always with you and will never leave you. Example today.

February 14, 2012

From St. Paul's ministries:

July 22, I was en route to Washington, DC, for a business trip. It was ordinary until we landed in Denver for a plane change.

As I collected my belongings in the overhead bin, an announcement was made for Mr. Lloyd Glenn to see the United customer service representative.

I thought nothing of it until we reached the door to leave the plane and there, eight people were asking every male if they knew a Mr. Glenn. At that point, I knew there was something wrong, and my heart sunk.

When I got off the plane, a settlement-based young man came toward me and said, "Mr. Glenn, there is an emergency at your home. I will see you through a telephone to check on the hospital." My heart was pounding, but the will to be calm took over.

I followed this stranger to the telephone. I called the number he gave me for Mission Hospital. My call was put through the trauma center, where I learned that my three-year-old son had been trapped underneath the automatic garage door for several minutes and then when my wife had found him. He might have been dead.

CPR had been performed by the neighbor, who is a doctor, and the paramedics had continued the treatment. Brian was transferred to the hospital.

Heartbeat had been revived. However, they have no lead yet as to how much damage had been done to his brain or to his heart. After speaking with the medical staff, my wife started weeping, but not hysterically, and I took comfort in her comments. On my ride back, the traffic lights seemed to last forever but finally, I arrived at the hospital. Approximately, six hours after the garage door had come down. When I walked into the intensive care unit, nothing could have prepared me to see my little son lying so still, running great big bed tubes and monitors everywhere.

He was on a respirator, and I watched my wife, who stood astride to give me a reassuring smile. Brian was going to live. The primary test indicated that the heart was okay, miracles in themselves. Only time will tell if he was brain damaged. All that night and the next day, Brian remained unconscious.

On this very day, at two o'clock that afternoon, he regained consciousness and sat up and said, "Daddy, hold me," he reached for me with his little arms. By the next day, he was pronounced as having no neurological or physical defects. The story of his miraculous survival spread throughout the hospital.

In the days that followed, there was a special spirit about our home. Our two older children were very much closer to their brother. My wife and I were much closer to each other, and all of us were very close as a whole family. We felt deeply blessed. Almost a month later of the accident, Brian woke up from his afternoon nap and said, sit down I have something to say. During this time, he was only able to speak in small phrases, so to say something in long sentence surprised my wife. She sat down with him on the bed, and he began his sacred and remarkable story.

"Do you remember when I got stuck under the garage door? Well, it was so heavy and it landed on me really bad. I called to you, but you could not hear me. I started to cry, but then it hurt so bad. And that's when the birdies came." "The birdies came"?

February 21, 2012

My wife was puzzled about the birdies. "They made a whooshing sound and flew into the garage. They took care of me."

"They did?" "Yes," he said. "One of the birdies came and got you. She came to tell you, I got stuck under the garage door." A sweet, reverent feeling filled the room.

"They flew up so fast in the air. They were so pretty and there were lots and lots of birdies." My wife was stunned. Brian went on to tell her that the birdies had told him that he had to come back to life and tell everyone about the birdies. He said they brought him back to the house until the big fire truck and ambulance were there. A man was trying to bring back the baby that day, and the birdies tried to tell the man that the baby will be okay. The story went on for an hour. He taught us that the birdies were always with us but we don't see them because they put something to block our eyes, and we don't see them. We listen with our ears, but they are always there. "We can only see them here." He put his hand over his heart. The spirit was so strong yet lighter than air. My wife realized a three-year-old had no concept of death and spirits, so he was referring to beings who came to him from beyond as birdies because they were up in the air like birds that fly. "What did the birdies look like?" she added. Brian answered, "They were beautiful. They were dressed in white, or some of them had green and white. But some of them had on just white." "Did they say anything?" "Yes, during that incident, they told you, your baby is lying on the garage door." He went on. "You came out and opened the garage door and ran to me. They told you to, 'Stay with your baby, and do not leave.'"

In Mark 2:1-12, we see more angels this time in the form of the paralytic's friends. The paralyzed man quickly got the help needed with the aid of others, it was that them who changed the paralytic's life forever. Oh, and a three-year-old Brian was saved from certain death by his birds.

Well, have you been an angel lately?

You stay with a sick child. Spend some time with grandma the Jew. Offer to babysit so your parents could go by themselves. And listen to your child tell you about their lives without interrupting.

Angels have many forms. They are individuals we can see, people like me and yourself who can help make another human being's lives better, like the good friends of the paralytic man.

Now, what lesson can we learn from this? We can learn that the Holy Spirit and Jesus are always there if we look for them. We can be kind to everyone. We can care about others. We can do things for one another. We can allow one another to be who he or she is, and we can accept them no matter how we feel. If we love, we can all become better people. Let us be an angel to one another, let us have compassion for one another, and let us care for one another. And most of all, have faith in Jesus, and miracles can happen and we can move mountains.

February 15, 2012

When I got up this morning, I said my morning prayer. I learned all about forgiving your brother. Here is part of Psalm 139. Out of the depths, I cry. Oh Lord hear my voice and Your ears be attentive to the sound of my pleading. You, oh Lord. Mark out my guilt, Lord. Who could survive without you? With you I found forgiveness. For this, we revere you.

See now, if you have faith in Jesus, He will forgive all sins.

Now back to what happened this morning. Deanna asked me why I was making those funny noises. I told her I was falling again. Every time I get unsteady on my feet, I make those noises. Jesus, please help me not to do this. I must find a way. Please help me. I know that you will. Jesus, what causes me to do this is it my medication? Is it the side-effect? Some of my medication probably need to be corrected. I must go now. It is time for me to go to mass.

Deanna and I just got up from eating a great lunch. The name of the restaurant was Friday's.

I was just thinking about how nice it would be to move out of this house, in a place just enough for us. We do not need this big house, do not need the responsibility of the tenant. Neither one of us is getting younger. I realized I have said this before, but it bears repeating. I need to check into getting my hip replaced in this left hip, and I'm now going to rest.

At times I feel that I am very bored, so I fail to trust. I sometimes feel that I can't be of any use to anybody or do anything for others. Once again I play the pity party, feeling sorry for myself. I cannot drive because I cannot drive. That is the way it is. I cannot change this. The fact that I cannot drive has nothing to do with my character. I still am a wonderful person. And I do count and I do matter. With the help of Jesus, I realize that everything I do in life and everything that happened to me happens for a reason. It is very important to know that what had happened in the past is true, but it is not who I am. So let's get over it, Gene, and let's get on with your life.

It is very important that I realize that my brothers and sisters are no better. Just because they may have more than me, having a good spiritual life is much better than having things of the world. To realize that you have Jesus, you need nothing else. It is nice to have material things, but you don't have to have them; they do not define who you are. Scott has called Deanna, and it made her feel very happy. Remembering about the gift certificates she gave them.

I got out of my resting. Deanna was making sandwiches. Things like this are the reason I love her. If only she would realize this; this is where she has beautiful qualities about her. She will do anything for anybody. She has a wonderful, wonderful character. I must also learn to do that when I dictate into this machine, I must speak slowly and clearly, just as if I was having a conversation with someone. This is going to take practice and training, which will be for a long time. I will get better.

I will now say evening prayer.

February 18, 2012

Well, yesterday was not a good day. I slept most of the day. I was not feeling good. My wife, Deanna, wanted to go to Charlie Brown's with Richard. He promised to take us to dinner. I was not doing well, but I did not want to disappoint Deanna. Because of my not driving, I cannot take Deanna anyplace. I feel very bad that I cannot. I do wish things were very different, but it is not my fault. I cannot blame myself just because it can't be done. It is better to accept my future life. It does not define who you are.

When we got back from dinner at Charlie Brown's, I was not feeling well, so I went to bed. In the morning when I woke up, I got very dizzy. It is probably because of my medication. I took some different medication to loosen my bowel. I could not go to the bathroom right. It may have been the combination of the medication I take on a regular basis with the added medication I took for my bowel movements.

This whole business created a huge fight between Deanna and me. It was not very pleasant. We did not do anything but blame each other. "Perhaps this time get a divorce," I said to her. There should be love between two people and there was nothing left for us. Of course, I started feeling sorry for myself and started to play a big pity party.

Things seemed to get better, and Deanna made breakfast. So we really do love each other no matter what is said. Jesus, I still need help. I am making all these funny noises. I am still using foul language that should not be used. I fell once again, something I have had for years. It was a case with the umbrellas and rightly so. Deanna was very angry. Whether I fell or not, I must take responsibility for the action.

Yesterday, I went to a meeting with my spiritual director. We talked about many things, all about what was happening in my life. I told her that. I was to have a strong faith and how blessed I am for Jesus because I know He will never leave. I shared with my spiritual director Mary Joe that my greatest challenge is selling the house; however, my wife Deanna does not agree with me. As I have stated beforere, neither one of us is getting any younger.

We do not need a monster of a house and do not need tenants. We also do not need the responsibility of having to maintain this house.

We also talked about my book. I learned that when you write a book, it does not get completed overnight; fix it about a year or so. Even if the book is never published, it is good therapy for you. But I know, Jesus will get me through with it.

It's a very good thing to learn. It's okay for you to write slowly.

Jesus, help me stop this hollering. Jesus, please help me not to use inappropriate languages. It serves no purpose, it would only worsen the problem.

This kind of language only hurts others, especially my wife, Deanna. There is no need for this time. Jesus would help me this, I know.

It is now time for evening prayer. God bless and peace.

February 19, 2012

Today, when I got out, I went out to get the paper and came back in. The paper for Deanna I left in the bathroom for her to read. I came out and put the coffee on and put up the window shades. Then I went to the bathroom to wash; I came out dressed. Just shortly after I finished dressing, I became very, very dizzy. I was supposed to go to Morristown for my oblate meeting. However, because I felt groggy and wobbly, I decided not to go to the meeting. The best thing for me to do was to stay home.

I did find the reason for the dizziness. What I had done was I had not put the correct medication in my pillbox. That is what made me dizzy. I corrected the problem, and the dizziness went away. I must be careful when I put my medication in my pillbox for the whole week. I must find a way to correct this problem. Deanna did not want to go, so very wisely I took the advice. Funny, I just had to take the microphone off because my ear was itching. A microphone that is. So now we're back in business, I must continue.

Now I was speaking of my medication. This time I was very careful and put it in correctly for next week. Every day I'm watching carefully with the help of Jesus. I did not say my morning prayer because, by the time I stopped getting dizzy and ate breakfast, it was then nine o'clock, and that was too late to say my morning prayer. My wife, Deanna, then went to mass. I went online to see if I can find a mass in audio, but I could not find one. I shall try to find one later. I am feeling much, much better now. But in order to keep from being dizzy, I must always, always remember to take my medication correctly. With the help of Jesus, I can do this. I started my contemplative prayer. This is where you slowly contemplate. You pick a reading from one of one of the psalms from the Bible. You repeat this five times, and each time you meditate. One reading at the time, each time you will find that the reading of the scripture affects you deeper and deeper. If you listen to yourself carefully, you will find that the reading tells you about what is going on in your life. It is a very, very powerful prayer.

What I said was my Lectio Divina. This prayer is for Ash Wednesday, the beginning of Lent. Lent is the forty days before Easter. During Lent, you abstain from meat, do penance, and reconcile your sins. After the forty days is over, we have Easter Sunday, which commemorates the resurrection of Jesus. He remains on earth for forty days until Pentecost. This is where the Holy Spirit ascends upon the apostles. We then go back to ordinary time until the beginning of Advent. This is the start of a new church year.

It is wonderful to see how my faith gets stronger. I did not know I was going to share all these. This is where your faith gets strong as well as your prayer life.

I have just thought of how I can make my falling a joke. You see, it is the floors coming up to get me. It is moving and is trying to attack me as well, and I have a four-prong cane that holds all the floors down as well as the moving chairs. So you see, it is not my fault. Look, just fix the moving chairs and tables, to hit me. You must be able to make fun of yourself. This type of attitude will keep you through life. This is why life is so awesome and wonderful. This is where you care for people. This is where you get the compassion, to love each other unconditionally.

All of this writing, all these are not about me. It is not about my writing the book. It is about you loving it. If everyone else is not there, I would never make it. We all support one another, we do count, and we do matter.

If we take responsibility for who we are and what we can do, then remember this always, we can move mountains. This morning when I got up, I encountered many problems. As you read the above, you can see where I turned bad into good. And I did not even know I was going to write this. Isn't this amazing?

I will now say my daytime prayer. Peace and God bless. Have a blessed day.

February 20, 2012

This morning I got up and got dressed. I took my morning medication. I went outside and got the newspaper for my wife. I came inside and into the bathroom to wash my hands and face. After that, I got dressed and went out to say my morning prayer. All of a sudden I got really dizzy. What I found is that it was from my medication, which was not taken right. Of course, Deanna was very upset, and I don't blame her. I decided to call the pharmacy to find out why I have the dizziness. They explained to me that perhaps it could have been my blood pressure medicine. He suggested that I take the blood pressure medicine in the evening before I go to bed. So effective tonight, I will take the blood pressure medicine before I go to bed. I was talking to my friend Peter. He took blood pressure medicine that night, and he said the same thing that Dave from the pharmacy told me. More than likely, because of my taking the medication inappropriately for a long time, this may have caused my falling all the time. So now since I am taking blood pressure medicine at night before going to bed, let us observe what will happen.

I sat down until the dizziness was over. It was about ten o'clock, and it was too late to say my morning prayer. Because I was unable to go to church or mass, I decided to see it online, so I did. Then my wife, Deanna, came in from grocery shopping, and I went to her to help her. I did something wrong because I did not hear her rightly, so she was very, very angry at me. I cannot blame her.

Well, let's change the subject and go back to writing my book. You know I have learned a very important lesson about myself. I do not have patience. My hollering, my getting upset, my anger, my making funny noises are part of who I am as a person. Now, since I have learned of this as being a part of who I am, I realize I am can change this. I will now go eat lunch.

I know I can trust Jesus to help me with this problem. This is a problem that I struggle with almost every day. It may be something you dislike, but because suddenly you realize it is part of you, you are able to correct it from bad to good. So you see? We can find value in this. This is how you can help another person who is going through the same circumstance. First, you have to let them realize who they really are especially the negative side, and have them accept all of it, and then they can now correct themselves. And it becomes a lesson of value to them. Things such as these are ways we can help one another. We all must have strong faith, and remember, Jesus will never leave us. You can count on that one.

Last night I realized that this book I am writing will take years. It finally sank into my brain, I have been making excuses. This is the first time, I have ever tried writing a book. And with the help of Jesus, it can and will happen. I must learn to be patient.

I was just thinking that since I now realize that I should look at each medication intently and read each bottle and make sure that it goes in the right slot. It is a good possibility that I will no longer have the seizures if I take my medication properly and accurately. I may stop using a four-prong cane and perhaps go to a single cane, and this will be a blessing.

Jesus, I have another problem, one that I know you will help me with. My left leg hurts me very much, and I somehow need to stop the pain. Once the pain disappears it would really help to keep my cool at all times. This will help Deanna also not to get upset with me. Jesus, please ensure her that I am really trying to stop this illness and that I'm not just acting this out. Help her believe me.

I need your help, Jesus, that I may realize that I should take Deanna seriously. That is not part of who she is. I must learn to accept this in her. Let me now say my daytime prayer and then rest.

God bless and peace.

I just thought of a good "should, could, would."

I should have years ago, taken my medication appropriately.

I should not have forced myself to a lot of driving, convincing myself that I can drive like anyone else.

I should not have driven distances.

I should have been more careful. If I did all these things, perhaps I would be able to drive today.

Why did it happen? Was I not careful?

Now, since all these things had been done and I cannot turn the clock back, what I can learn from it, is not to do it again. And I can help someone else not to go through what I did.

So you see the value in this is to be able to teach others not to do the mistakes I did. To tell others that it does not hurt to do this.

And most of all, the right thing to do is to allow these things to happen to you. No matter what they are, you let them happen. You cannot undo what the past has done to you, but you can improve on it. So you see what I have done, others do not have to do them. They can learn from me and grow as I did.

God bless and peace.

I got up this morning. I went to the bathroom to wash and get dressed. I logged in to my computer and said my morning prayer. I'm taking blood pressure medication for high blood pressure. It does not seem to be working because I'm still getting dizzy, which means my blood pressure is high. I think I do need a change in my medicine. I will go to the doctors tomorrow to have it checked out. A few days ago, I was taking blood pressure medicine in the morning. Then I was told by Dave from the pharmacy to take the blood pressure medicine in the evening to see if it would get better after a short time. I once again got dizzy. And I will see him tomorrow.

James 4:1–10: Beloved, where do the wars and where do the conflicts among you come from? They come from your selfish desires that are at war in your bodies, don't they? You want something but do not get it, so you commit murder. You covet something but cannot obtain it, so you quarrel and fight. You do not get things because you do not ask for them!

You ask for something but do not get it because you ask for it for the wrong reason—for your own pleasure.

You adulterers! Don't you know that friendship with the world means hostility to God? So whoever wants to be a friend of this world is an enemy of God. Or do you think the Scriptures means nothing when it says that the Spirit that God caused to live in us jealously yearns for us? But he gives all the more grace. And so he says,

"God opposes the arrogant but gives grace to the humble."

Therefore, submit yourselves to God. Resist the Devil, and he will run away from you. Come close to God, and he will come close to you. Cleanse your hands, you sinners, and purify your hearts, you double-minded. Be miserable, mourn, and cry. Let your laughter be turned into mourning, and your joy into gloom. Humble yourselves in the Lord's presence, and He will exalt you.

Mark 9:30–37: Jesus and His disciples left there and began a journey through Galilee, but He did not wish anyone to know it. He was teaching His disciples, telling them the son of God made man and needed to be handed over to men and they will kill Him, and three days later after His death, the Son of Man will rise, but they did not understand what He was saying, and they were afraid to question Him.

They came to Capernaum and, once inside the house, began to ask them, "What were you arguing about and why?" But they remained silent for they had been discussing among themselves who was the greatest. Then he sat down, and called the 12 and said to them, if anyone wishes to be first he showed me last and he shall be last of all the servers. He took a child placed him in their midst and put his arms around him and he said to them whoever receives one child such as this in my name receives me whoever receives me receives not me, but one who sent me.

Now, what is said about us in this gospel, is said in whatever order we are in, first or last we are all equal we should care and love one another. Yes, we disagree and we think one is better than the other, we must realize that this is not the case. That we should care and have compassion and love for one another. We are who we are because we are who we are. We love one another because we love one another. No one is equal because no one is equal. Tomorrow is Ash Wednesday, forty days before Easter. Where we fast and do penance for our sins.

There are several things we can do. The Lenten season is a time of penance, a time of reconciliation, a time for prayer and for helping those less fortunate. Visit those in hospitals and nursing homes and so many other places. Lent also teaches us to grow stronger and with the help of Jesus become a much better person. You know the most important thing that I got out of this was a sharp lesson of prayer, a stronger faith, and to strengthen my everyday attitude. I am going to rest now. Peace and God bless.

February 22, 2010

I got up this morning, got washed, and dressed. I ate breakfast. After having breakfast, I said my morning prayer. Today is Ash Wednesday. At about nine o'clock, I went to the doctor for my blood pressure. Today, everything was fine. The doctor just changed my medication. So far I have not been dizzy. My wife, Deanna, has been wonderful to me today. She is a very wonderful person. I just wish she allows herself to realize this. I do wish she would not make herself wrong.

I have been thinking, it's about my strong faith. It is a good way to start the Ash Wednesday, which is the first day of Lent. Jesus, I am still doing the following: the lack of patience, the inappropriate language, and the hollering, and also the swearing. I still need all the help I can get with this problem, so I can change this part of who I am. I know it is part of who I am now, but all this swearing, all this hollering, all this lack of patience needs to be addressed. Jesus, I really do need to stop this because it does not seem to be working. I have promised Deanna that I would improve, but it is not happening. I know that I am growing from this but, Jesus, please show me how I'm going to become a better person by this.

Genesis 9:8–15:

God told Noah and his sons, I solemnly promise you and your children and with every animal that is with you, of these birds and cattle and wild animals. I will never again send another flood to destroy the earth. I set this promise with a bow in the clouds as a sign of my promise until the end of time to you and all the earth. And it shall come to pass, that when I bring a cloud over the earth, that the bow shall be seen in the cloud: and I will remember my covenant that is between you and every living creature of all flesh, and the waters shall no more become a flood to destroy all beings.

Peter 3:18–22:

I paid a visit to see you for a possible road to heaven which your fathers tried to take the Prince and he lives to Christ not mere gold or silver you very You very well know. Review with this precious lifeblood of Christ sinless spotless lamb long before the world began only recently once the war into public view in these last days as a blessing yourselves because of this. Your trust in me thinks who raised Christ from the dead and gave him great glory now your faith in him alone now you have real love, everyone, because your souls have enclosed selfishness and hatred we trusted to say you stole it. You really do love each other warmly with all your hearts.

I see how strange life is. I never knew I was going to obtain these verses of the Bible. The things that I got from the Bible and the verses are to love and care for one another from our hearts.

What we get from Lent are reconciliation, prayer, and almsgiving.

Now on a totally different matter, I need from now on to watch my medication. Very carefully I must read from each bottle what kind of medication it is I am supposed to take and when to take it.

Whether it is for the morning or at night, I must be careful. Jesus, would you please help me with this?

I will now say my daytime prayer and then go rest. God bless and peace.

February 23, 2012

After getting washed and dressed, I came in and said my morning prayer. After breakfast, I took my medication. About an hour and a half later, I started getting very dizzy. When I went to the doctor's yesterday, he changed my medicine, and I did not think it was why I was having trouble. So I changed it back to the way it should be, let us try to find out tomorrow if it works in the morning. Right now I'm thinking of how blessed I am, and that things could be much, much worse. It is a beautiful feeling to be able to feel good about myself. Despite all that has happened to me in my life, I am so fortunate that I have a place to stay, a roof over my head, an amazing wife, Deanna, and wonderful grandchildren. A lesson I had learned from reading the Bible, like the verses taken from Genesis 1: Peter, it gave me a great sense of joy for doing almsgiving and forgiveness.

I am very fortunate that I have had no seizures. However, the game is not over yet. My goal is to have no seizures ever again. On another matter, I still even have to stop the improper language that does not work, have a lot of patience, the constant hollering that does not work, and to respect Deanna. Obtaining all these things can and will make me become a better person. You see, if we never give up, we can all maintain the caring and having compassion for others. Being compassionate and loving and caring are qualities that will not be forgotten. I am now thinking that Deanna went out and bought me a new case for the medical needs required of me to use. Because of my dizziness, I was unable to go to mass so, I went to mass online instead. Hopefully, when I take my medication tomorrow morning, I will be able to take the right one and the dizziness will go away.

I received an e-mail from Tom Stuff, Oblate Coordinator. Tom would like to send us out and find new Benedictine oblates during the season of Lent.

It just came to my mind that I must always remember to put my earphones on every time I think of making my diary for my book. If I do not fix up everything around me, I'm having earphones cuts whenever outside, so I should do it appropriately. Oh, I'm just thinking about my support group for epilepsy that meets every last Thursday of the month. Will I be able to get a ride? Or is it over for me because of the fact that they do not drive? Should this be the case? I will miss it very much because helping those people with seizure disorder like I have, is very important to me.

I will say my daytime prayer and my contemplative prayer and then go to a restaurant.

Peace. God bless.

February 24, 2012

Good morning, all. It is a rainy day. Not too uplifting. It was unfortunate for me today, as I got dizzy still from the medication. I had to sit down until the dizziness went away. I was told by the doctor that this dizziness where all as soon as the medication. I now will go eat my lunch.

Jesus, I still need help with my mouth, my hollering, my pounding, my patience, and my making funny noises. Jesus, it does not seem to cease. Please show me a way to stop all this business. I have a strong faith that you will. This does not work in my life. The only thing it does is hurt Deanna and I would certainly choose not to. Deanna has had enough.

Okay, now on a different note. I said my contemplative prayer, my Lectio Divina. What I got out of it is trusting Jesus. I also understand the concept of sin and how the devil tempts you. There is sadness all around us. You go to the store and you see magazines hidden. You see disguised pictures of women inappropriately dressed. You see sexy, negative women. This is totally inappropriate and is very, very sinful. These are some of the ways that will tempt you. During Lent, we have what we call the Sacrament of Reconciliation in which you can be forgiven. Always remember that no matter what, the Lord will always forgive you and Jesus will never leave you.

You know I had a real challenge today. I received in the mail the suction cups that I ordered for my grabbers. This is where my lack of patience, my hollering, my pounding, and my swearing started. For some reason, I cannot seem to stop this. I have not discovered a way to stop it. I know this is part of who I am, but when you realize you can change the habits you have, especially the bad ones, then you should do it. It will just take more prayers, a stronger faith, and the will of not giving up. For some reason, I'm starting to wonder about my brain surgery. I am thinking about how it affected my memory. Because of this, my book will be very repetitious since they really did a number on my memory. Isn't it strange, how stuff comes up in your diary? Stuff that seems to be out of place or would have nothing to do with writing it down in a journal. I was also just thinking of the pity parties I used to buy, and the way I was bought into them.

You see, this is where I grow when I am able to look at these pity parties played by me and realize the value I see in them.

I have not had seizures this January. This is the longest I have gotten without having a seizure. Give me another three months, and I'll begin to have some hope for not having another seizure. As long as I take my medication, probably this can and will happen. I just now remembered that I was not able to go to mass today, so I went online. I did find a site where you can have daily mass every day real-time instead of being one day behind. This is a very important thing as it strengthens my faith and prayer life. Having all this faith and a strong prayer life helps me to have no seizures.

This is where having the surgery affects my memory. I was just writing something down, and I completely just lost it. You see, these types of things are the kind of things that make me angry when I am writing something down and forgetting it instantly what I was about to write. Oh well, life goes on. Six points down the road, I will remember it like it was yesterday.

Deanna does not realize that I am writing a book about my life, it seems to her that I am just sitting and playing around with my computer. But I must allow Deanna to be who she is, and she is and always will be a wonderful person even if she doesn't think so. Deanna is everything for everyone. I will now say my daytime prayer and then rest.

I have just said my evening prayer. There are few more things we need to do during Lent; that is to visit those in prison, to care for the sick, and to care for one another. Since I am unable to do this because I do not drive,

I will pray for them that they would be given the strength and to trust in Jesus. This is how I can be with them spiritually.

Scripture reading, Romans 6:3–5, 9/11: Do you not know that all of us have been baptized into Christ Jesus were baptized into His death? We were buried therefore with Him by baptism into death: so that Christ was raised from the dead by the glory of the Father. Even so, we also should walk into newness of life. What if we have been made with Him in the likeness of his death? We shall certainly be united with Him in the likeness of his resurrection.

What we know is that Christ, being raised from the dead, will never die again. Death has no longer power over him. That he died to sin once and for all, but the life he lives is for God. So you also must consider yourselves dead to sin and alive to God in Christ Jesus.

Psalms 117:1–9, 13–19:

Give thanks to the Lord for He is going, for His love endures forever, that the sons of Israel say His love endures forever. The sons of Israel say His love endures forever, the sons of Aaron say his love endures forever, and those who fear the Lord say, his love endures forever.

I go to the Lord in my distress. He answered and freed me the blues at my side. I do not fear what you meant to say against me; it is better to take refuge in the Lord than to trust in princes.

I was thrust, thrust down to falling, but the Lord is my helper. The Lord is my strength and my song. He was my savior. There are shouts of joy and victory in the tents of just

Lord's right hand has triumphed his right hand raised me up the Lords left hand and strength. I shall not die. I shall live to recount His deeds.

I was punished. I was punished by the Lord but not doomed to die alternatively the case of holiness

I will answer and give thanks. This is the Lord's own gate when they just may enter.

I will thank you for your answer, and you are my savior. The stone that the builders rejected has become the cornerstone. This is the work of the Lord, a marble in our eyes. This sale was made by the Lord. Rejoice and be glad.

Oh, Lord, this salvation has only been a success. Blessed is he who comes in. The Lord will bless you for the house of Lord the Lord God is our light.

0h, we're in possession with wrenches over to the altar. You are my God. I thank you, my God. I praise you. Give thanks to the Lord for His love endures forever.

This Psalm is very appropriate for Lent. It shows how much the Lord loves us and cares for us. Let's follow Jesus always. He is our hope and our salvation, so let's trust in Him. Let us close by saying the Our Father. Our Father who art in heaven, hallowed be thy name. Thy kingdom come. Thy will be done as it is in heaven. Give us this day our daily bread, and forgive us our trespasses as we forgive those who trespass against us. But lead us not into temptation, but deliver us from evil.

Soul of Christ, be my salvation. Body of Christ, be my comfort. Blood of Christ, wash out my sins.

Jesus Christ, my comfort be now and at the hour of our death. Amen.

Gee, this is my diary,

February 25, 2012.

Strange. The first thing that came to my mind was when I was working for the Board of Education of South Plainfield.

That summer we were working at a school. I was working on a scaffold, putting lights, and I was not too swift as a person, and the other person on the scaffold was just as dumb as I was. We were told that it was the blind leading the blind, and believe me, it was.

Then I was in another school, and I felt like using a scrubbing machine. I was in middle school, and I was asked to wax what should have been cleaned already.

My point is that these things happened many, many years ago, and I remember them as if they were yesterday. I think because of my surgery it has affected my memory. This is the way it turned out. I believe I explained this in a previous chapter. There are so many other things that happened that I can share with you, but there are too many of them.

Well, I am just waiting. I said my morning prayer. During Lent, you maintain a strong prayer routine. You see your reconciliation. You see the strength of that prayer I give you.

And you didn't know the medication for my blood pressure. I became very, very dizzy. This is going to continue until the new medication holds off.

I just ate breakfast that Deanna made for me. Deanna also put out my clothes as she does every morning for me.

Deanna is an admirable person. I will always love her.

I will be back as I am going to say my contemplative prayer (Lectio Divina). I was able to do my contemplative prayer. This prayer is when you read a psalm and concentrate, allowing yourself to experience it. How does Psalm apply to me? For example, Psalm 117, reading it midway spoke to me to praise the Lord and trust in Him. I can always count on Him being there for me, and on what I can do.

It is amazing to be able to experience and know that Jesus is always with me, and He will never, never leave me. I do trust Him. What a remarkable experience if you have this trust.

I just received a call from the publishing company asking me if I would like to submit my materials. They wanted me to buy another program. I told them that this is the first time I have ever begun to write a book, so I am not ready to submit anything.

I am going to write this book very slowly. No one will try to rush me. Because this is my first time, I do not know whether this will make it or not. I can only do my best. The book may never be published. That is my present feeling, but I know that deep down it will work.

I go from sitting, looking out the window, wondering what I should say next. My mind is now blank.

God bless and peace. Have a blessed day.

February 26, 2012

Today after breakfast, the dizziness came back soon. With this, I did not go to church. Perhaps this dizziness will go for good after the medication kicks into my body. It is very unpleasant to have this feeling. It only holds me up. It is too bad I could not find the first Sunday of Lent online. Perhaps I cannot do it because the of way things are set up. In any event, I am still thinking about a lot of history I have regarding when I started to be a Benedictine monk when I had to leave because of my epilepsy. My life was devastated. I did not know where to turn. I do believe I explained it in a prior part of my diary.

I worked for a collection agency. It was fine for epilepsy, but I worked with Dean Witter and company. I was also fired for epilepsy. After that, I was fired from the Catholic school system. I do not remember where. I then worked at Muhlenberg hospital. This is the only job I did not get fired from. After I worked at Muhlenberg hospital, I worked for the Board of Education in South Plainfield, New Jersey. I remained there until I retired. What's strange to me is I am reminded of those in my present day.

I am also thinking about Notker. I can remember the story when I met him personally some sixty years ago when I finally went to Italy. I got to meet him in the

Benedictine, he is called the abbot primate; this means archabbot an equal to an archbishop. Notker and I still communicate through my computer.

What is important to me is the fact that I am a Benedictine oblate. An oblate follows the rules of St. Benedict. It is a very close group of people who care for and love one another no matter what. Deanna is wonderful. She is just making lunch.

The Bible reads in Genesis 9:8–15, "Then go to Noah and his sons. I solemnly promise you and your children and the animals you brought with you, all the birds and cattle and wild animals, that I will never again send another flood to destroy the earth. And I see all this promise with a sign. I place my rainbow in the clouds as a sign of my promise until the end of time, you and all the earth, when I send clouds over the rainbow, will be seeing the clouds, and I will remember my promise to you that every being, that never again will water destroy your life.

1 Peter 3:18–22: For Christ also hath once suffered for sins, the just for the unjust, that he might bring us to God, being put to death in the flesh, but quickened by the Spirit: By which also he went and preached unto the spirits in prison; Which sometimes were disobedient, when once the longsuffering of God waited in the days of Noah, while the ark was a preparing, wherein few, that is, eight souls were saved by water. The like figure whereunto even baptism doth also now save us (not the putting away of the filth of the flesh, but the answer of a good conscience toward God,) by the resurrection of Jesus Christ: Who is gone into heaven, and is on the right hand of God; angels and authorities and powers being made subject unto him.

Mark 1:12–1: the immediately the Holy Spirit led Jesus into the desert. He was there in the wilderness for forty days, tempted by Satan; and was with the wild beasts, and the angels attended unto him. Now after that John was put in prison, Jesus came into Galilee, preaching the gospel of the kingdom of God. And saying, "the time is fulfilled, and the kingdom of God is at hand: repent and believe the gospel.

So now all of us can see that Jesus is always with us and we should always remember to praise Him. He will always bring us from temptations and our sins.

Peace and God bless. Have a blessed day.

February 27, 2012

Today when I got up, it felt very strange. Today was somehow different. Strange, I do not know why.

Perhaps it was the fact that I was no longer dizzy from the medication for blood pressure medication given to me by the doctor. Perhaps it might have been some old thoughts. I was thinking of some things that happened to me with my family. For some reason, I remember loud and clear my sister Eileen going to the high school prom. It was raining that night. She was all dressed up in a beautiful dress. My father was teasing her, "Eileen, are you going to wear boots because it is raining." I was then thinking of what if we got caught when we broke a dining room chair when we had some friends over. That weekend we had some company, they were blamed for breaking the chair. Of course, the truth came out later, and we all got in trouble. I am never working for Joseph church's grocery store.

Why is it Lord that these thoughts from so long ago, are coming up now? Is it strange how thoughts of years ago come up on the blue? Sometimes your mind goes crazy.

Okay, now let's see if we can get back on track. I said my morning prayer. I did some of my contemplative prayers. I learned that if we help people in prison, those who are sick, those who are in hospitals, and those who are less fortunate than we are, we represent Jesus, every time.

Let us read the book of Exodus 6:2–13:

God said to Moses, "I am the Lord. I appear unto Abraham, unto Isaac, and unto Jacob but by name of God the Almighty, but by my name Jehova was I not known to them. I also establish my covenant with them, to give them the land of Canaan, the land in which they were living as strangers. And now that I have heard the groaning of the children of Israel, from the Egyptians treating them as slaves; I am mindful of my covenant. "There were the Israelites, the word that will free you from the forced labor of the Egyptians and will deliver you from their slavery. A rescue by abstract form, and with a mighty act of judgment, I will take you as my old people and you shall have me as your God. You will know that I am the Lord as your God when I free you from labor and bring you into the land I swore to give you, Abraham, Isaac, and Jacob. I will give to you as your own possessions, I, the Lord."

But when Moses told this to the Israelites, they would not listen to him because of their rejection and their hard slavery.

Then the Lord said to Moses, "Go and tell the powerful king of Egypt to let the Israelites leave his land. Moses protested to the Lord, "If the Israelites would not listen to me, how can it be that Pharaoh will listen to me for the speaker that I am?" Still, the Lord reined Israelites out of Egypt, spoke to Moses and unto Aaron, and gave them His orders regarding both the Israelites and unto Pharaoh king of Egypt, to bring the children of Israel out of the land of Egypt.

Okay now from this verse in the Bible, is asking us, do we ever listen? Let us listen to others who do not have it easier than we do, myself with my seizure disorder, people who have a disability, and those in prison, those in hospitals.

So you see, let us try to listen and be sensitive to the people around us. This is especially important during this season of Lent. So, let us care for others. By doing all of this, we become better people. In truth, this is who we are. This is what the entire book is about. It is all about trusting in Jesus.

Jesus, once again I need help with my anger, hollering, and getting upset. I was at my computer and something was wrong. Once again I lost my temper. This can and must be omitted.

February 27, 2012

Oh, I forgot to mention today. It was very, very hard to move the side table for one of our living room chairs. This is where my patience should come in. These are the type of things or the challenges you have during Lent.

Challenges will always appear after prayer. Always test your faith, and believe me, sometimes challenges such as these are real.

God bless, peace and have a blessed day.

February 29, 2010

Well, yesterday I was able to recall past experiences. So how did they get erased? I will now try to remember what happened. I know that I was in my office, and all of a sudden I had these peculiar thoughts regarding where I worked and one wherein I wanted to be a monk. I was in St. Paul's Abbey in New Jersey, New Jersey. I have a seizure disorder. I had to leave because of my epilepsy. My life was shattered. All I wanted to be is to become a monk.

When I did my contemplative prayer, I learned about forgiveness, caring for others, almsgiving, having compassion, and being patient.

Jesus, I still need help with my hollering, my patience, and my mouth. Dear Jesus, I do not seem to be stopping my lack of patience, my hollering, and my getting upset. The way I carry on is not fair to my wife, Deanna. She does not deserve this kind of treatment. Jesus, please help with my inappropriate language when I am with Deanna. There is no excuse that I do this.

Also yesterday, I had some frustration. Most of the day I was searching the Web, looking for a pay site table for my check. I finally bought one, which is a little more than I wanted to buy, but it did solve the problem. It took away my frustration.

Well, I guess that's l all I can remember about yesterday.

Now let's start today. I got up this morning. I said my morning prayer. I learned from it another lesson about trusting Jesus. I also discovered that you have emotions, you have anger, you have anxiety, you have lack of compassion, you have depression and many other negative feelings. But you see, all they are, are emotions. They do not define who you are. You must experience these feelings, but there is no need for you to hold on to them. After losing all of them, you can look at them, and as you do, you become a much better person. If you look hard enough, you will see the value in all of them. They are good and bad feelings and emotions. In life, no matter what state of mind you are feeling, you allow yourself to grow as a person.

The advantage of keeping a diary is that you are allowed to see your own daily growth.

February 29, 2012

This is today's Bible reading.

From the book of Exodus 10:21–11:10:

The Lord said to Moses; stretch out your hand forward to the sky, over the land of Egypt that there may be such intense darkness that one can feel it. And Moses stretched forth his hand toward the sky, and there was dense darkness in all of the land of Egypt for three days. Men could not see one another, neither rose any from his place for three days. All Israelites had light where they dwelt.

Pharaoh then summoned Moses and Aaron and said, Go and worship the Lord. Your little ones may also go with you. Only your flocks and your herds must remain. Moses replied, You must also give us sacrifices and burnt offerings, that we may sacrifice unto the Lord our God.

But the Lord made Pharaoh stubborn and he would not let him go. "Leave my presence," Pharaoh said to him, "You see to it that your face does not appear before me again. For if I see your face again, you shall die." And Moses said, "Then I will see your face no more"

Then the Lord said to Moses, "I will bring one more plague upon Pharaoh and the land of Egypt; after that, he will let you go. In fact, drive you away. Instruct your people that every man should ask his neighbor, and every woman, her neighbor, jewels of silver and gold. And the Lord gave the people favor in the sight of the Egyptians.

Moses then said, "Thus says the Lord: At midnight I will go forth to Egypt. Every firstborn in this land shall die, from the firstborn of Pharaoh that sits upon his throne, even unto the firstborn of the slave, and all the firstborn of the beasts. Then there shall be great wailing throughout all the land of Egypt, such as none like it. But against any of the Israelites and the animals. So that you may know how the Lord distinguishes between the Egyptians and the Israelites. All these servants of yours will then come down to me and prostrate for me. With that, he left the Pharaoh's presence in great anger.

The Lord said to Moses, "Pharaoh refuses to listen to you that wonders may be multiplied in the land of Egypt. And Moses and Aaron did all these wonders before Pharaoh: and the Lord hardened Pharaoh's heart so that he would not let the children of Israel go out of his land.

March 1, 2012

When I got up today, I went straight to saying my morning office. I learned that no matter how great we are, we always should honor Jesus, who was sent by His Father in heaven. From this, we learn to discipline ourselves. Then go to our Lord Jesus with whatever problem we have, and He will save us.

I had just been sharing with my wife, Deanna, about not acknowledging my seizure disorder. Everything I have done throughout my life—being fired from my jobs, my growing up with a seizure disorder, the way my family dealt with me, the way when I was in school, how the students stayed away from me because of my seizure disorder. Even when I totaled three cars, I was also a great burden to Deanna. My seizure disorder was the cause of all the trouble I had.

It's strange. What a diary does to your mind, things that happened many years ago, they become part of your life as you're writing your diary.

Genesis 22 1–2: Just as Abraham was put to the test to sacrifice His son, we are asked to sacrifice ourselves for the Lord.

In sacrificing ourselves to the Lord, we obey His word and He will take care of us always.

Today everything I do, whether the experience is good or bad, I offer it out to the Lord. He will always be there for me.

Mark 9:14.

I found this verse applies to me.

When he joined the disciples, he saw a large crowd around them and some scribes arguing with them. The moment they saw Him, the whole dropped with amazement and run to greet Him. "What are you arguing about?" He asked. A man answered Him, "Master, I have brought to you my son. There is a spirit of the dumbness in him. Whenever it takes hold of him, it throws him to the ground. He foams at the mouth, gnashes his teeth and becomes rigid. I asked your disciples to drive out the spirit, but they could not." "You faithless generation," Jesus said then, "how much longer must I be with you? How much longer must I put up with you? Bring him to me." They brought the boy to Him, and as soon as the spirit saw Jesus, it immediately threw the boy into convulsions. He fell to the ground and rolled around, foaming at the mouth. Jesus asked the father, "How long has this been happening to him?" "Since, childhood," he replied. "We have often thrown him into the fire and into the water in order to destroy him, but if you can do anything, pity on us and help us if you can." Retorted Jesus, "Everything is possible for anyone who has faith." And immediately the father of the boy cried out, "I do have faith, help me overcome my unbelief!" Jesus saw how many people were running to come around Him. He rebuked the unclean spirit.

As you can see, in Mark's Gospel, he speaks of a young child with a seizure disorder. I am using the language with regard to epilepsy, which we have today.

The old language is fit, epileptic, and convulsions. This terminology is even used today. We use the word seizure disorder because this is a much better term than in the old language. So because of my epilepsy, it definitely applies to me.

Let me see, what else has happened to me today? Today I had a man fix our chair that was damaged; he did an outstanding job. I was unable to go to mass today. I had a very good lunch, which my wife, Deanna, made for me.

March 1, 2012

Well, what else? I had a dream last night, and I learned that no matter what you think of, even if you do not know the day or the month, or what is happening around you or in the community, understand that Jesus is always there to help you.

Oh, Jesus, I still need your help with my patience, with my hollering. Once again, my wife, Deanna, does not need to be exposed to this. It is not my intention to hurt her feelings.

Exodus 12:1–20: The Passover

Yahweh said to Moses and Aaron, "This month is to be for you the first month, the first month of your year. Speak to the whole community of Israel and say that on the tenth day of this month, each man must take a lamb for each household. If the household is too small to eat the whole lamb, then they must share it with their nearest neighbor, you must take into account the number of people there. You are to determine the amount of lamb needed in accordance with what each can eat. The animal you choose year-old males without defect; you may take them from either the sheep or the goats. You must keep it until the fourteenth day of the month when all the members of the community of Israel shall slaughter them at twilight. Then they are to take some of the blood and put it on the sides and tops of the doorframes of the houses where they eat the lambs. That same night, they are to eat meat roasted over the fire, along with bitter herbs, and unleavened bread. Do not eat the meat raw or boiled in water, but roast it over the fire, with the head, feet, and entrails. You must not leave any until morning: whatever is left, you must burn it. You shall eat it like this, with a girdle around the waist, sandals on your feet, a staff in your hand. You shall eat hastily. It is the Passover of Yahweh.

The above is the Passover feast, which shows us that besides honoring Jesus, we should also celebrate for ourselves.

Peace and God bless and have a blessed day.

March 2, 2012

Jesus, I'm still having trouble with my patience and hollering. I was putting on my shoes and I started it again.

Jesus, please continue to help me. I need to stop this. There is no excuse for this.

Okay, what has happened today? I had a dream last night, something about a test. I did not understand it. Something about my father. He had a meeting and he gave me something to say at this meeting, but I cannot understand it. The priest asked me to talk to Father Casey. Why I cannot understand it, is because both my father and Father Casey are dead. This is weird. Perhaps it is something I saw about subsequent speech which the dream portrayed.

I got up this morning and said my morning prayer. I learned that we should always be thankful for what we have when things are good and when things go wrong, we immediately go to Jesus and ask Him for help. It sounds like we are very ungrateful children. We should always try to master how we feel. If we do this, we will have a strong faith and will even be stronger if we don't stop. Our houses will be peaceful and we become better people.

I have been seizure-free since the beginning of the year. It has been two months long that I have been without a seizure.

I'm not going to celebrate quite yet. Give me another six months and I will start getting happy regarding this progress. I need a ten Stations of the Cross. I had forgotten stations, so I recalled them as I waited for Gloria to give me a ride after mass. My wife, Deanna, came home with the groceries, and I helped her put it away. Then, of course, I went to mass. Deanna, as always, made me a wonderful lunch. I just happen to think, I should begin to train myself to read. I am hoping that my wife's set of prayer books will be the first step to accomplish this. By June, with these books, I'll be able to follow the daily mass with the priest.

Exodus 12:21–36:

Injunctions Relating to the Passover

Moses summoned all the elders of Israel and said to them, "Go at once and choose the animal for your families and slaughter the Passover lamb. Then take a bunch of hyssops, dip it into the blood in the basin, and put some of the blood on the top and on both sides of the doorframe. None of you shall venture out of the house till morning. Then when Yahweh goes through Egypt to strike down the Egyptians and sees the blood on the doorframe, He will pass over the door and not allow the destroyer to enter your houses and strike you down. You must keep these rules as an ordinance for you and your descendants. When you enter the land that the Lord will give you as he promised, observe this ritual. And when your children ask you, "What does this ritual mean?" you will tell them, "It is the sacrifice of the Passover in honor of Yahweh who passed over the houses and the Israelites in Egypt and spared our houses." And the people bowed down and worshipped. The sons of Israel then departed and carry out the orders that Yahweh had given to Moses and Aaron.

The tenth plague was that of the firstborn, and at midnight, Yahweh dropped down off the first one in the land of Egypt. The firstborn of Pharaoh, the pendulum is known, the first one of the prisoner in his dungeon, and the firstborn of all the cattle. Pharaoh the oldest countries and all the Egyptians The In the night, there was a great cry in Egypt, for there was not a house without its dead. And it was at night when Pharaoh summoned Moses and Aaron. He said, "You are the sons of Israel, and get away from my people. Go and offer to Yahweh as you asked to bring the herds and go. And also ask a blessing on me." The Egyptians urged the people to hurry up and leave the land because, they say, "Otherwise we shall all be dead." So the people carried all their dough still unleavened, on their shoulders, their kneading bowls wrapped in their cloaks.

March 2, 2012

The Egyptians plundered the sons of Israel. As Moses had told them, ask the Egyptians for silver ornaments and gold for clothing. Yahweh gave the people such prestige in the eyes of the Egyptians, that He gave them what they asked, so they plundered the Egyptians.

So you see, on this verse from Exodus, no matter what happens to us, what we do, Jesus is always with us and will never leave us. If we open our Bibles and read at least one verse, we will see how much we can grow.

I will now say my daytime prayer. Peace, God bless and have a blessed day.

March 3, 2012

Well, today I got up, I started my morning prayer, and I ate my breakfast. Okay, let's start the day with my diary.

Today I began with a little anger with regard to my not being answered regarding a ride to the self-help group on epilepsy. I have done all I can to ask for a ride. I have sent messages on my cell phone, trying to get a ride to the meeting, without success. So I guess going to the self-help group is now out of the question. I will miss them, but life is like that sometimes. I must not forget what is behind me and go on with my life.

Today, I read my Lectio Divina, which is a kind of prayer wherein you will concentrate slowly on a verse from the Bible. You read it, listen to the verse, and see how it applies to your life. You will discover that if you contemplate and internalize the verse, you will be able to discern how it applies to your life.

It applies to me today. Always trust in Jesus. I was going to write a letter and share my disappointment with not getting a ride to the meeting, but the Lord told me that I do not have to share to let it go because by writing it down in my book, I have done this. There is much more to life than wasting your time trying to make a big bang of this matter because you are playing a pity party, pity parties don't work for you. You can cut off all communication just by not communicating again.

This is where writing books help you with your life. You can express in a book what is going on with you because a book does not talk back to you.

My leg hurts me very much, my left leg. I do my exercises every day. This does not seem to help. My appointment with Dr. Geller has been changed. I was still able to maintain my appointments with Dr. Geller. He is a doctor I see about my brain surgery, which I had February 17, 2004. It is strange how I remember that as if it was yesterday. I wonder why I think I know, ha-ha.

I am now thinking about my family, Deanna, and all the people around me. Do they really believe that I can make this book happen? I can't predict the end. We'll make it happen with the help of Jesus. Jesus never lies to anyone; He will never leave me. As I write my diary today, I realized what it feels like to be able to help others who are also going through the same experiences as mine. They should not see this as a setback, as I did grow up with epilepsy. It is nice to be able to do this. This is one more reason you get to grow and become a better person. As I am writing this diary today I just felt that Jesus is with me.

March 3, 2012

I have just thought of two powerful prayers:

Our father who art in heaven, hallowed be thy name. Thy kingdom come on earth as it is in heaven. Give us this day our daily bread.

And forgive us our trespasses as we forgive those who trespassed against us, and lead us not into temptation, but deliver us from evil.

Hail Mary, full of grace, the Lord is with you.

Blessed are you among women, and blessed is the fruit of your womb, Jesus.

Holy Mary, mother of God, pray for us sinners, now and at the hour of our death. Amen.

Let me now go read a book. Perhaps I can, and continue with my diary afterward.

March 3, 2012

Today, I just thought about when I joined the Plainfield ski club. They had a ski lodge in Killington, Vermont. I took up the sport, and it was very, very nice. This is where I met John L. I then began to live this style of life. I justified this by the fact that when I was in the monastery, I was studying to be a monk. I lived with men. I did leave the Catholic Church, but I never left religion.

I then started to go to gay bars. I lived the gay style of life for a number of years. I did stay with skiing. I learned to ski appropriately. I went to school in a place called Gray Rocks located in Canada by Brother Roger, who lives in Oregon. Roger invited me out. Well, one of Roger's friends was an expert. He taught me how to be a better skier. I also went to see my brother Jerry who lived at that time in Chicago. I also skied in Switzerland at Mount Vermont. Back home I skied at Park City, Utah.

At one of the gay bars, I met a Frank Stevens. We became gay lovers. I moved with Frank to Stocken, New Jersey. This only lasted a year because it did not work out.

I then became very, very sick with my epilepsy. It was so bad that they were going to have me admitted to the hospital. This is where my mother and father were there for me. It was then I changed back to the straight life.

I then felt things were back to normal. I live in South Plainfield. I went back to Sacred Heart Church in South Plainfield and started singing in the choir, leading the people at mass. I started to go to a divorced and separated group at St. Luke's in North Plainfield. This is where I met Deanna. We became very good friends and then married. Isn't it strange?

When you write a diary, things come up automatically from the past.

I never dreamed I was going to come up to a point of sharing my past life. I have some years later, but I guess that is when life stinks on you when you least expect it. It really amazes me how a diary does this.

The difference is you can look back at the stuff that used to run your life. As you look, you can perceive how you are able to correct yourself by looking at your past with a much different eye or perspective and grow and really become a better person. Things that used to tear you apart, you are now able to see the value and grow. You cannot undo what has happened, but you are able to grow to become a better person.

You learn that Jesus is always with you. He even got you through your past. I did not realize it, but Jesus was there giving the strength and helping me to have faith in Him and forgiving me even when I had done that. With my diary, I was able to share so much for the first time today. Diaries are really amazing, are they not?

Peace, God bless and have a blessed day.

March 4, 2012

Well, today I am still disappointed regarding not getting a ride to go to the self-help group on epilepsy.

I am now able to put it behind me. Life does go on.

Today I got up and said my office of readings and my morning prayer.

Today is the feast of the Transfiguration, for our Lord Jesus was transfigured before Peter, James, and John. Six days later, Jesus took them with Him and led them to a high mountain where they could be alone by themselves. They were in their presence; He was transfigured: His clothes became dazzling white and whiter than any earthly bleacher could make them. Elijah to them with Moses; and they were talking with Jesus. Rabbi, he said, "It is wonderful for us to be here. So let us make three tents. One for you one, for Moses, and one for Elijah." He did not know what to say; they were so frightened. And a cloud came, covering them in the shadow, and there came a voice from the crowd. "This is my beloved son. Listen to Him." Then suddenly, when they looked around, they saw no one with them anymore but only Jesus.

Now how do you think this appears to us today? Think of when you're driving a car and it stops working. You do not know what to do. Will my wife come for me? Will she get help for me? The cars around me are very upset. I am very upset. You do not know what to do or where to go. Suddenly everything changes. Your wife comes to help you and brings AAA to help with your car. You no longer fear what was happening. You are able to move along with everything.

You can know how James, Peter, and John must have felt the time of the Transfiguration. If we live in the present, not the past and not the future. We live in the present moment. We see the Transfiguration every day of our lives. You never know what is going to happen. When living in the present, you can be transformed every day of the week. If we look at life, you can see the experience I had today by reading. By not getting a ride to the self-help group, I was disappointed. I felt I had been let down and deceived. But after that experience, I was able to let go of it and get on with my life. So you see how I was transformed? It happens to me every day of the week. Compare this to the value I see when I look at my past, good, bad, or indifferent. He is mighty powerful, is He not?

I realized today as I am writing in my diary that I have grown even more as I continually become another person.

Right now, what is flashing up is all my experiences of my entire life, what has happened to me, how I felt.

The pity parties I played, the way I felt sorry for myself, because of my epilepsy I was not able to take the SATs, not being able to go in the army and not being able to go to college. Yes, this was unfair to me. I felt my family and people did it to me, but tell me now, who bought into it? I do believe it was me. So I do believe that Gene must take some responsibility. It does not excuse whether I could do it or not, does not excuse me from being responsible for this. So you see transformation even applies here. It is ironic to think that on the feast of the Transfiguration, this entire experience is thought of as one of the things that came up today in my diary. This is how Jesus works every day of my life and allows me to be who I am, who I truly am. I pray every day that I will continue to maintain my commitment, my strength, and prayer. From this diary, you can see that Jesus never leaves me and never will. He is always present.

The power of Lectio Divina is a traditional practice. Initially, we need to acquire the discipline of close reading and attention to every word and sentence, and not allow ourselves to pass over anything. To be this consistently disciplined it would really help by reading out loud the verse and to articulate it well. You vocalize words slowly while avoiding distraction. Lectio is like reading poetry; the sound of the words creates inferior assonances, which, when working, turns a trigger condition. Connections that are a lot more effective in the memory. In Lectio, the intention is not cognitive. It is a work of the heart that desires to make contact with God and thereby reform our lives. It can help us sidestep the questions that would otherwise dispense our energies. This preparation is not Lectio, but it serves it well.

Attention to the ambiance of our Lectio will often help us more smoothly into prayer. Like choosing a place or an environment located where there would be no disturbances. Your posture will also aid you in praying properly without discomforts. Using an icon offering reference to a book of Scripture will often help us to move into a more prayerful space. This explanation is from one of the rules of St. Benedict. I do this kind of prayer every day of my life.

March 4, 2012

I will now say my evening prayer.

God bless and peace have a blessed day.

March 5, 2012

Last night I had the strangest dream. I had a dream of getting my teeth fixed. After that, I was dreaming that I got my medical alert bracelet for my epilepsy, that I broke it. For some reason, instead of trying to fix it myself, I tried to take the bracelet to a jeweler or a key shop to somehow get the bracelet fixed. I could not make any sense with this. Strange what dreams do to you.

Because I lost my ride to the self-help group on epilepsy, I started my own group on Facebook and Twitter. I hope we will be successful in having a new group for brain surgery on epilepsy.

Today I am beginning to experience transubstantiation. Since I did not have a support of my own I think I can form one in a different way. Jesus, what I need help with now, is to create my own website. Let me know how I can do this. The idea formed in my wanting to start afresh, something new. Look how I was transformed.

Just as our Lord saves Moses from the Egyptians, Today we can be saved from the devil by trusting in the Lord. We need this trust every day of our lives. For some reason, I do not know why I just started to think about how I feel bad with regard to helping in church with the readings, helping with serving, being unable to help in church. This is because of my epilepsy. I do not understand their feelings about my having epilepsy. I do think of what it comes from is when I have something called status epilepticus, which is Latin for "state seizure." I do think of Father George's experience and fear in seeing this status epilepticus. I have tried to explain that this does not matter. But when Father George and everyone else gets this in their mind, they cannot let go of it. They cannot live in the present. They have a great fear of me because of my epilepsy. But I know that epilepsy is not something I have. Jesus, could you somehow inspire Father George and all the others to accept this and allow me to help them? Jesus, this would help me very much in making my faith even stronger to be able to contribute, to somehow feel that I count. I know that I do count. I just need you to allow them to see the same thing that I do.

Please help me despite everything to maintain my presence in any way I look at. Now my thoughts are going through my head about things that happened to me in the past that I do not know where to start. I am now thinking about when my sister Eileen shared with me, how she looks at me and tells me what life is, telling me the things and what I have been dealt with. I am able to have the ability of strength and faith not to give up.

March 5, 2012

Support such as this gives me the strength and the strong faith to carry on. My life is all so valuable to me.

Psalm 37—a major part of my life.

Do not fret about the wicked. Do not envy those who do wrong. For like the grass they wither, like green plants, they will die in the field.

Trust in Yahweh and do what is good. Make your home in the land and enjoy peaceful pasture.

Leave rage aside and turn away from wrath. Do not agonize, nothing but evil can come.

From Psalm 38:

Yahweh, do not punish me in your rage or reprove me in the heat of anger. Your arrows pierce deep. You hand has pressed down on me.

Because of your wrath, my health has failed. There is no soundness in my body because of sin. While guilt is overwhelming me, it is too heavy a burden.

My wounds are festering and are loathsome, because of my sinful folly. I am bowed down and brought to my lowest; all day long I go about mourning.

My back is filled with searing agony, there is no health in me.

I am weak and utterly crushed; I groan in anguish of heart.

My friends and companions shrink from my wounds; my neighbors stay away from me.

Men intent on killing me lay snares. Others hoping to hurt me talk of my ruin.

Lord, do not forsake me or be far from me; Come quickly to help me.

But no matter what, Yahweh is my prayer if I trust in Him.

I can apply what is said in the Psalms to my own life. If I look intently enough, I can see my failures in a different light. If I look at the value hard enough, I can feel myself grow to be a better person.

I say to people, "Stay away from me and do not hurt me." But do you see, if I look at it, who is really hurting me? It is me not taking responsibility. So here I can look at the one responsible for actions. This is once more is transubstantiation playing a role in my life even today.

Peace and God bless.

March 6, 2012

I saw the wisdom.

1 Corinthians 1:22–25:

The jurors consider Jesus to be foolish because they were trying to hammer Him into the mold that they had created of what the Messiah looked like back then. Since He didn't meet their expectations, they thought He had no significance.

Both the Jews and Greeks considered the crucifixion to be criminal and said that Christ's crucifixion was wrong—that because of this event He was a valueless fool.

Many people, past and present, think that Jesus was foolish because He came as a humble servant of His father and the human race.

Power, influence, and wealth which has eternal value?

Loving our neighbors as yourself for the Jews demands signs, and Greeks seek wisdom but to those who are called, both Jews and Greeks. Christ crucified is the power of God and the wisdom of God.

In our own lives, we see the wisdom and we see insight. But when we look back, we do not have both. We do not have to see the Lord Jesus Christ, through His crucifixion, He has saved us. In our eyes, the crucifixion is valuable to us as it gives us the strength to carry out our lives.

Once again we see the Transfiguration. We can see the transformation. It brings us reconciliation for the forgiveness of our sins. It also helps us to see how we can help people around us no matter what they do or how we see them in. They know it.

I also saw my wife Deanna not wanting to continue fixing her problem. She will not go to the hospital. She feels that the doctor will not help her. Jesus, please tell me what I can do to be of some value to Deanna.

To be able to help her with this, she needs to take care somehow. Strangely, this morning, I had a dream regarding Jimmy, my son.

Deanna asked me if I was in touch with my son. I called my son.

We made plans to go camping somewhere. I also broke the alert bracelet I have for my epilepsy; it alerts people so they can tell if something happens to me during accidents or emergencies and if I have a seizure.

March 6, 2012

I have just finished. The doctors checked my blood pressure, and everything is okay.

My mind is mixed up. I am thinking so many things. A time with family, my wife Deanna, my son James, and where they fit in my life. It has come to my mind also, my working experience. I asked myself why I am thinking of all of these today. There must be a reason. I cannot put my finger on it.

I guess it just is because it is.

I am now thinking about my prayer life and the strength I gained, the faith I have in Jesus.

Once again I am thinking of anger, depression, anxiety, frustration, not having patience. I also realize that these feelings are nothing more than emotion. Yes, you must deal with them, but they are not who you are. You are wonderful. All the experience, if you let them go, they make you realize you do matter, and also, you do count. This, in turn, makes us care for one another. It makes others have compassion for each of us. Jesus helps us to see all this. It also gives us strength and faith.

I see myself, the wisdom I gained from my experience of doing my Lectio Divina. This is the prayer where you contemplate, and slowly read a passage from the Bible.

I have just opened the Bible, and my eyes went to verse 29 Isaiah against tree worship. Yes, you will be ashamed of terebinth, which gives you such pleasure. You will for the gardens that will charm you, since you will be like a terebinth with faded leaves, like a garden without water.

The man of high will tinder His handiwork. A spark both will burn together, and no one will put them out.

Everlasting peace

vision Isaiah 7 and Amoz concerning Judah and Jerusalem.

In the days to come, the mountains of the Temple of Yahweh shall tower above the mountains and shall be listed higher than the hills. All the nations will stream to it. People without number will come to it, and they will say, "Come go up to the mountain of Yahweh, to the temple of God of Jacob. Teach us His ways so that we may walk in His paths. Since the law will go out from Zion, the oracle of Yahweh, He will wield authority over all the nations and adjudicate between many peoples.

Their swords into plowshares.

Their spears into sickles nations will not lift up sword against nation there will be no more training for war.

O house of Jacob, let us walk in the light of Yahweh.

So you see, all the wars we have today, no matter where they are—Iraq, Vietnam, and all other wars—if we trust in Jesus and follow Him, we will have everlasting peace.

March 6, 2012

March 7, 2012

Today I have finally discovered how to make my book a direct number of pages.

I talked to the publisher today. He told me to set a number that would work for me.

So I said to myself, I will not go over two hundred pages. This way the diary can stop. Because it is a diary, it is not set on forever. He also recommended regarding awards, just to put a couple in of the important ones and leave the others out.

When I said my office, I have learned once again that if we trust in the Lord, there is no fear. Psalm 39:

I said, "I will be watchful of my ways and keep my tongue from sin; I will put a muzzle on my mouth when the wicked man stands before me.

I remained silent, not even saying anything good. But my grief increased, my heart was burning within me. While I meditated, the fire blazed up; then I spoke with my tongue:

"Our Lord, show me my life's end and how short is the length of my days; let me know how fleeting it is. My life for you has given me a short span of days. My lifespan is nothing in your sight. A mere breath, even to those who stood so firm.

Everyone goes around like a mere shadow; in vain they run about, heaping riches, not knowing who will have it in the end.

And now, Lord, what is there to wait for?

My hope rest in You, set me free from all sins because this was all you want.

Take away your scourge from me.

I am overcome by the blows of your hand. You punished man's sins and corrected him. You devour all his treasures, mortal man, no more than a breath; the Lord, hear my prayer.

Oh, Lord, turn your ear to my cry. Do not be dead to my tears in your house. I am a passing pilgrim, like all my fathers. Look away from me, that I may relish life again before I get on to be no more.

Do you see how our life is, in this psalm? Every Psalm tells us that Jesus will never leave us. We can always, always count on Him. If we put our trust in Him, he will keep us always.

Now let's have a little fun.

I did some research for my book. This is what I found: All these seizures, being in a coma, and having status epilepectus, I was banging on the doors to get into heaven. This is neat, isn't it?

Yes, they may have been very serious problems, but don't we have to loosen up? Life is much too short to take things seriously.

I will now say my daytime prayer. God bless and peace.

March 8, 2012

I wake up this morning and was thinking why?

All I do is sleep. Am I active? Am I doing this on purpose? I do not seem to go anywhere.

I cannot take my wife, Deanna, anywhere. Deanna is not really feeling too good. The doctor and a pharmacist cannot understand what is going on with Deanna. I just hope that she begins to feel better.

And also, Deanna never stopped weighing herself down. She never seems to give herself some credit. She is an astounding person. She does amazing things to a lot of people. I wish Deanna would allow herself to be who she is.

She would be a much better person if she would acknowledge all that she has done. I love Deanna very, very much. She is someone I shall never forget. Deanna is a remarkable person. If she would only allow herself to realize how much people love and care about her. Not everyone is like Deanna, who will leave someone's lunch for him or her. Deanna has so much to give. If only she would realize this herself.

I just noticed in the first paragraph the huge pity party I was playing. Now in the second paragraph, I can see how I have changed. I have given Deanna an opportunity to show how wonderful she can be and is.

If she would only allow herself to be who she is. I have also realized that I love Deanna and shall never forget her.

So you see, you can change your pity immediately. With the help of Jesus, all can happen.

I am somewhat lazy. Yes, I do sleep because I need to, but I should not use this to play a pity party. I can use my bad qualities to look at myself and make myself grow and become a much better person.

Psalm 44:

We heard it with our own ears, O God; our ancestors, have told us the story of the things you did, in days long ago

You planted them, where You have uprooted the nations; You crushed its peoples and made our ancestors flourish.

No sword of their own won the land. No arm of their own brought them victory. It was your right hand and the light of your face, for you loved them.

It was you, my King and my God, who granted victories to Jacob.

Through you, we beat our foes. You will bring foes to shame all day long. Our boasting was in God, and we praise your name without ceasing.

March 8, 2012

Even now you have rejected us, disgraced us.

You no longer go forth with our enemies. You made us retreat from the foe.

Our enemies plunder us at will.

You make us like sheep for the slaughter and scatter us among the nations. You sell your own people or not and make no profit on the sale.

You make us taunted by our neighbors, laughingstock of all near among the nations. You make us a byword among the peoples. A thing of derision all day long. My disgrace is before me. My face is covered with shame at the voice of the tauter, scoffer, at this site of the foe, the avenger.

Do you see that even today, if we are destroyed in any of our adventures today, be it good or be it bad, our Lord Jesus Christ, His father, and the Holy Spirit will always forgive us?

I was very glad to see that my wife, Deanna, was able to buy a nice dress. I was very glad to see that Deanna was able to get what she wanted today. You know, when I read Psalm 33, I realized the power and the strength it gives me, and it reminds me to continue with my prayer, thereby giving me stronger faith.

I am now going to lie down and rest. Peace and God bless. Have a blessed day.

March 9, 2012

Today I got up and said my morning office once again. I learned to trust in the Lord. Jesus gives me strength. He gives me faith in Him. He is always with me and never make me feel alone.

I opened my e-mail and got a letter from Kathy. She is a very good friend of mine. She asked about my wife, Deanna. However, I do not share this with Deanna because she does not feel that Kathy and I are just friends. Deanna still fears that Kathy and I have a stronger relationship, and this is not true.

What happened last night, I had a bad and strange dream, Deanna went someplace with my family. Apparently, we were traveling someplace in Pennsylvania and staying somewhere there. We would stay overnight with a family there. I cannot understand this. Apparently, I was still working, and somehow, I got myself in trouble because I wanted to leave and go to Pennsylvania. Now, first of all, it was not that my family was misplaced in Pennsylvania. I do not know where this place is in Pennsylvania. I am not working. I am retired.

Perhaps this may have been a combination of things that my wife Deanna had talked about, different things. She talked about her family in Connecticut. I talked about my trips, going skiing, and other trips that I have made. These are the only things that Deanna and I talked about, so I guess this may relate to the dream I had.

Then Deanna told me she was going to go to the grocery store and asked me if I would wait for her and help her with the groceries. She said that no one else helps her. I think that Deanna always wants to complain. She will never be happy. I guess she knows nothing else because she was put down in her prior marriage. I think that is why she fears that Kathy and I somehow will have sex. This will never happen, but Deanna will never believe this.

Now let me see, what else has happened to me today?

Oh, I was thinking today about the time when I was on the underside of the fence, when I was gay.

As I have said before, the entire story has come up. Should I put this in my book? Is he too strong? Should I put it in at all? He is part of my diary, but in the book, what the books sell. I am going to ask George if I should put him in there. Or should I ask my sister Pat? I have just called Patty, and she will get back to me when she can. Patty is the only one I can trust with this, "my past life."

I have told Patty that she can and will get a job. Always trust in Jesus. He will never leave you.

Jesus answers your question no matter what. Never forget you're a wonderful person and also very kind. You have always been there for me, and I shall never forget your friendship. You're one person that I go to if a problem occurs.

I am just thinking that March is a very bad month for Deanna. She has her granddaughter Christina who has her birthday. She has her daughter Kim who had a heart attack. These are just a few things she has in the month of March, which makes this one very unpleasant for Deanna.

Peter has called to take me to mass today.

When I came home, my wife, Deanna, was disappointed. She wanted me to look in the catalog to get slacks from Blair. She also said that she gets help from no one.

March 9, 2012

I just got up from a good nap. Somehow I'm going to learn to speak correctly into my microphone. Somehow I must enunciate words correctly. I must speak appropriately into the microphone. It should be about one inch from my mouth. I do believe that the process is complete.

I will now say an evening prayer.

Peace and God bless and have a blessed day.

I must now learn to accept that I will have seizures.

I was hoping this would be possible at some time. Taking my medication correctly does not seem to work. This morning I was not able to take my medication the way that I should because of my having seizures. I do wish I could make this happen, but it just will be never possible.

Jesus, say this will not be possible, to be free of seizures. Please give me the faith and the strength to be able to accept this fact. As much as I do not like it, I must accept it. I feel very bad that my wife, Deanna, must accept this. She has been wonderful about this. Deanna is not well herself. She has been through so much with what she has, and I only add to it. I am not being very fair to her. And we are not having an easier time. Sometimes life is like that.

Exodus 20

Jesus, I still have faith in you. Please show me and give me the strength to get through this.

I have a huge headache. Every time I have a headache, this is an indication of the seizure.

I'm so tired right now. I have slept most of the day. Of course, things could be much, much worse regarding my seizures. What I do not like is my wife, Deanna, having to do with this. She has always been wonderful to me. I shall never forget. Jesus, please help me with my spirits. They are very down today. I need someone or something to uplift them.

Exodus 20:1–17:

Then God spoke all these words: "I am Yahweh, your God, who brought you out of the land of Egypt, out of the house of slavery. You shall have no gods except me. You shall not make yourself a carved image or likeness of anything in heaven or on earth beneath the waters under the earth. You shall not bow down to them or serve them. While I am Yahweh, your God, I am a jealous God and I punish the children for the sins of their fathers, to the third and fourth generation of those who hate me and show kindness to a thousand generations of those who love me and keep my commandments. Remember the Sabbath is a holy day. For six days you shall labor with work. But the seventh day, Sabbath, for Yahweh, your God, you shall do no work on that day. Either you or your son or your daughter nor your servants doing the animals even the stranger who lives with you. For in six days, Yahweh made the heavens, and on the seventh day, He rested. That is why Yahweh has blessed the Sabbath day and made it sacred. You shall not kill. You shall not commit adultery. You shall not steal. You shall not bear false witness against your neighbor. You shall not covet your neighbor's house. You shall not covet your neighbor's wife or a servant, man or woman, or his ox or his donkey, or anything that is his.

March 11, 2012

Now let's apply this verse from Exodus to our own lives. Now we see that there is no other God we must adore other than Yahweh. If we accept this, all is possible for us. Let us trust in Jesus and He will guide us through life.

Today I had a seizure. I did not like it. Yes, it was small; nevertheless, I am going to maintain and have faith that Jesus will help me through this mess because I would rather not have anything.

Jesus will help me do this if I have faith, but it must remain strong.

I will be going next week to my oblate meeting. I will be able to share how much I have done with my book.

Today I have shared with my wife, Deanna, that we should get rid of this house. Things would be much, much easier on both of us. Neither one of us is getting any younger. We do not need the responsibility of having a tenant or having the hassle on this monster of a house. However, it is unfortunate that Deanna will not move. I could only make this happen. Things would be much easier on Deanna and me. Jesus, is this want you want too?

Because if this is your plan, then I will also accept this. Please guide me as to what I should do.

I trust you will.

Oh, I meant to share that yesterday, March 10, I slept all day because of having a seizure. The seizure made me very, very tired, so I was unable to write anything. Today I feel much better.

I have just discovered today that I made a terrible, terrible mistake with the publishing company. I should not have thousands of dollars to print the new book. The publishing company, unfortunately, when I called, thought I was an expert. How do I correct this? I must speak to Judy, the person that takes care of me now. I think that she takes care of pros only. I am far from a pro. I'm a beginner. Perhaps I need to get someone else to help me with the book.

I also need to straighten out where I got the $3,000 from. Did I get it from the bank? Did I get it from the account that Deanna and I made together?

Jesus, another thing you must help me with once again is my sounding off all the time. I'm always hurting Deanna's feelings. It is not fair to her that I sound off all the time. This is a part of my character that needs change.

March 12, 2012

Today I got up and said my morning prayer (office of readings). I learned about keeping the Ten Commandments. Deanna and I went to the bank straighten out some money, and we got that finished. After we were finished, Deanna went to the store to get some groceries. I stayed home and had lunch.

I had no seizures today. I know the seizures are not serious; however, I do not want to have any, not even the small ones. Jesus, please help me with this problem. I would like for you to help me obtain this.

I am still getting angry, sounding off at Deanna. She does not need this. She's upset enough. Today I am wondering if I should stop my book or if I should I continue to do one.

March 12, 2012

I also say tried to get my cell phone to have a different tone.

2 Chronicles 36:14–16:

Furthermore, all the heads of the priesthood, and all the people too, added infidelity to infidelity, copying shameful practices of all the nations and the defiling of the temple that Yahweh had consecrated for himself. In Jerusalem, the God of all their ancestors tirelessly sent them messenger after messenger since He wished to spare His people and His house. But they mocked the messengers of God and despised his words they laughed at His prophets until at last, the wrath of Yahweh was so high against His people that there was no further remedy.

You know what we get from this verse? That we listen to our Lord and trust in Him and only Him. If you read this closely and will let it build in your hearts, you will really realize that any verse in the Bible always applies to us. If we trust in Lord Jesus, He will send the Holy Spirit to protect us always. You can see that this affects all people, which means, let us trust one another. This will allow ourselves to let everyone to be who they are.

March 13, 2012

Today when I said my morning prayer, I learned all about forgiving others.

Well, this morning I got a haircut. I was unable to attend mass because I forgot to call Gloria in time.

About a week to ten days ago, I bought a side table. It has not arrived yet. So I tried to get the name of the company. I tried searching for it, but I could not find the name. So I finally gave up, so what I am going to do is just to wait for it to come.

After I got my haircut, I then had lunch that Deanna made for me. I would just call for supper.

March 14, 2012

Today I got out. I said my morning office. I learned that if you obey our Lord, He will reward you and affect you. After getting dressed, I read verses of the Holy Bible (Lectio Divina). This is the type of prayer where you contemplate and allow your mind to go slowly so you can find out how the verse of the Bible applies to your life.

There are so many thoughts that go into my head today that I do not know where to start. Is my book going to work? Will people like it? This is my own diary of my everyday life. Of course, I know that with the help of Jesus, I have no fear that it will work.

Exodus 33:7:

Moses would pitch a tent at some distance away, outside the camp. Anyone who wished to consult the Lord would go to this meeting tent outside the camp.

Then Moses said, "You let me see your glory!" He answered, "My Presence will go with wherever you are and I will give you rest."

March 14, 2012

But my face you cannot see, one always sees and still lives. For here continued, "There is a place near me where you shall station yourself on the rock. When my will set you in a hollow rock. When my glory passes new, I will set you in the hollow of the rock and will cover you with my hand until I have passed by. Then I will remove my hand so that you may see my back, but my face is not to be seen."

Now let us see how we apply this to our life today. Even though we cannot see our Lord, He will always be with us no matter what we do.

Now, what just came to my mind is that I must always remember my medication, especially for my seizure disorder. Somehow I must start reading books and also newspapers, keep myself informed of what is going on in the world.

I am now going to rest.

Peace and God bless and have a blessed day.

March 15, 2012

Today I said my morning prayer, I then said my Lectio Divina, the type of prayer wherein you concentrate slowly on a verse of the Bible. You allow the verse to see how it applies to your life.

What I found was that if you trust in the Lord and receive Him in the Holy Eucharist, you gain much more strength and a greater faith. Let's see what I'm thinking about today. How much more does my sister Eileen, after my mother's death, seem to get more of the money from my mother? So you see now, the pity party I am playing. It does not really matter to me because that is the way it's.

Now let's get on with it, Gene. Life goes on.

We must always remember that we are that counts more. We have no time to feel sorry for ourselves. As long as we have Jesus, He will bring us through all things. Today I have helped Deanna with dusting my computer and the shelving around it.

March 15, 2012

I will now get ready for mass.

I just finished helping with some ham for my wife, Deanna. She wants to cook it for Saturday, St. Patrick's Day, and she would like to have Wayne over for supper.

Oh, wait, who is going to take me to Morristown, to St. Mary's Abbey, to my meeting for the Oblates?

The Oblates are a group of people who follow the rule of St. Benedict and are a very close group of people who care for one another. As I have stated at one time, I was going to be a Benedictine monk. I had to leave because of my seizure disorder. The oblates sort of makes up for them. I'm not becoming a monk. Because now I can follow the rule of St. Benedict.

Once again I am thinking about the comparison between my sister Eileen and me, but this time I realized I'm able to let this go. Look at it and see that it makes no difference no matter what. I still can become a much better person, and a stronger person might be able to look at this situation and grow from it. In everything I see and do, whether it is good or whether it is bad, I just get stronger and gain more value for myself.

So do you see how wonderful life can be if you allow it? No matter what you are thinking, no matter how you feel, no matter what people say or do to you, you learn that it's the people that have the problem and not you. Once you do not feel good about yourself, try to find what it is all about, experience it (the feeling), and grow from it.

Always remember that Jesus is always there for you. He will see through it all. Always remember how wonderful you are, and never forget life is awesome, and I am not being funny.

I am now going to say my daytime prayer. Peace and God bless and have a blessed day.

March 16, 2012

Now this morning when I got up, I said my morning prayer. I learned that our Lord, Jesus Christ, is always with us and always forgives us. You will see in today's readings in Ephesians 2:4–10 and John3:14–21.

Because God so loved us so much he was generous with his mercy: He made us alive with Christ even when we were dead through our sins. It is through grace that we have been saved and raised up with Him and gave us a place with Him in heaven in Christ Jesus. This was to show for us ages to come, to His goodness for us in Christ Jesus, how infinitely rich is His grace. Because He is by grace that you have been saved and raised up to date, not by a gift from God, not by anything that you have done so that nobody can claim credit. We are God's work of art. We are in Christ Jesus to live the good life he had met us. From the beginning, he had meant us to live

March 16, 2012

So now do you see? How when we do not want to follow Jesus or we do not want to follow His law. All we want to do is follow our own free will. And to do our own thing and do what pleases us alone. He loves us as we are. Now here's what happened to me today. I'm still swearing, I'm still hollering, I still have lack of patience. Jesus, please give me the faith, the strength I need. Jesus, I still need help with this.

John 3:14–21:

As Moses lifted up the serpent in the desert, so is everyone who believes be lifted up and have eternal life. Yes, God loves the world so much that He gave His only son, so that everyone who believes in Him may not be lost.

I may have eternal life. For God sent His only son into the world not to condemn the world, but so that through Him the world might be saved. No one who believes in him the command; one who refuses to believe is condemned already because he had refused to believe in the name of God's only son. On the grounds, a sentence pronounced that. The light has come into the world men have shown for darkness to the light because they're the word evil. And everybody who does wrong hates the light and avoids it, for fear his actions should be exposed, but the man who lives by the truth comes out into the light so that it may be plainly seen that what he does is done in God.

So you see if we believe in Jesus, who died for us, if we choose the light and not the darkness, and we should always live the truth.

Now today I went to the stations of the cross, and it was very powerful for me to experience this. This year in the season of Lent, I have had unusual and powerful experiences I have ever had. For some reason, my prayer life has become very powerful. It is have given me the strongest prayer life and the strongest faith I have ever had. I have noticed in my life today that I can accept everything that I am going through.

I'm just thinking about today. Is the book that I'm writing going to work? This book is my first try. With the help of Jesus, it will work for me.

Oh, Jesus, I just realized that I love and a catalog today, and I was looking at something I should not have been looking at, and that was some stimulating sexual enhancements. Jesus, this is where I need your help and your forgiveness. Kindly help me to steer away from this. This is totally inappropriate for me to ascertain.

Last night I texted my entire family to see if they were all okay. Some answered me and some did not. And that is okay with me. I am now going to rest.

Peace and God bless and have a blessed day.

March 17, 2012

After reading my morning prayer, I did my Lectio Divina. This is the type of prayer wherein we contemplate slowly and allow your mind to see how the verses of the Bible apply to your life.

Today is St. Patrick's Day. I wonder if I should call my publisher regarding my book, just to touch base with them and find out what is the length of an average book. This is my first time. I have never done this before. I am thinking about my brain surgery and how it applies to writing my book. I'm sitting here trying to decide how to organize my thoughts so that I can put them in my diary today. I have a symbol. It is an Irish fish. He is a symbol for recognizing Jesus Christ. The fish are two nails together. What I did discover is that they recognize your Christian faith.

I am now thinking about organizing my finances, and when I get my money at the end of this month, I will be able to invest the entire two checks from Social Security and my pension fund in a different mutual fund. Once it is there, I can no longer take it out. I do not need that much money in my money market, and this will make me more money. I also must be careful of the way I spend the money. Oh, my wife, Deanna, just showed the sweatshirt from Cape May that I had blood on; it all came out. That was awesome! I thought that I had ruined it. Today Deanna made me a wonderful breakfast. Oh, I just happen to think that the self-help group that we had for epilepsy fell apart.

What I am going to do is get a chat line on Facebook. Finally, I am learning to be able to pronounce appropriately and slow enough that Dragon now picks things up. I have now found out that with the help of Jesus, this will is going to work. Also, Deanna will always be there for me. She is a wonderful person.

With my prayer, my faith, my strength, and the help of Jesus, this can and will happen.

I also must not continue this business of making noises, this constant hollering and also my lack of patience.

Jesus, please help me bring this to a stop.

John 3:14–21:

"God so loved the world He gave His only son," Jesus said to Nicodemus, and Moses lifted up the serpent in the wilderness. "So must the son of man be lifted up, that whoever believes in Him may have eternal life."

For God sent His son into the world, not to condemn the world, but that the world might be saved to Him. He who does not believe in Him has been condemned already. It because he has not believed in the name of the only son of God.

This is the judgment that the light has come into the world, and they chose darkness rather than light, lest his deeds should be exposed.

Let he who does what is true come to the light that made it clearly seen that his deeds have been wrought in God.

March 17, 2012

So you see, no matter what we do, the good, bad, or indifferent, Jesus is always there and will always love us. That is very reassuring.

March 19, 2012

Today is the feast of St. Joseph, husband of Mary, Mary who is the mother of Jesus. It is a very important piece of the church.

Yesterday, March 18, there was nothing written in my diary. More than likely because I had an oblate meeting at St. Mary's Abbey in Morristown, New Jersey. An oblate is a group of people that will say and read daily a rule of St. Benedict. It is a very close-knit group. Yesterday I saw a tape of Edith Stein. She was a Carmelite nun who was taken by Nazi German. She was taken to prison where she died.

I am going to share with you a little bit of information regarding the Carmelite nun. Edith Stein was a saintly Carmelite nun, a profound philosopher, and a great writer. She had a great influence on the woman of her time and having a growing influence on the intellectual and philosophical circles of today's Germany and the whole world. She is an inspiration to all Christians, whose heritage is the cross, and her life was offered for all Jewish people in their suffering and persecutions.

Pope John Paul II beatified Sister Teresa Benedicta of the Cross on May 1, 1987 and canonized her on October 11, 1998. Learn from St. Teresa to depend on God. God will fill you. With only joy, courage, and strength, St. Teresa shares with you to always depend on God.

It seems that St. Teresa has told me this already, because all through my book, this is what I share with you. So it feels like she has told me already without me even knowing her. What an experience this is for me.

It is strange. I am now thinking about my family and how fortunate they are that they have more than me. Okay, now let's stop. This is the beginning of one of my pity parties. Now, let's get on with it. Life is much too short.

Life has been so wonderful to me. I am able to accept it with the help of Jesus. He had never left me, and I can always count on Him. In a few minutes, I will be going to mass. When I come home, I will eat my lunch and say my Lectio Divina. This is the type of prayer wherein you contemplate and read slowly a scripture the Bible. After which I shall continue with my book.

After mass, I was invited to participate in a program that will help you welcome people into the parish. I was quite honored to be asked. Jesus, please help me to explain to Deanna the importance of me doing this. Please help me to keep my cool regarding this matter, which Deanna understood that I really want to do. I love people.

March 19, 2012

Jeremiah 31:31–34:

I will make a new covenant and remember their sins no more.

"Behold, the days are coming, says the Lord. I'll make a new covenant with the house of Israel and the house of Judah, not like which I made with their fathers when I took them by the hand and bring them out of the land of Egypt my covenant which they broke, though I was their husband

This is the covenant which I will make with the house of Israel after that time, says the Lord "my law within them and I will write it in their hearts; and I be their God and they shall be my people

No longer showing each man, each his neighbor, and each his brother, saying Know the Lord or they shall know me, from the least of them to the greatest, for I will forgive their iniquity and how I will remember their sin no more."

These verses of the Bible tell us to review the time Jesus endured the ungrateful, that we did not get the gifts we expect.

Have you read the diary? In my book, you will see parts of my life that I suffered, and because of Jesus, I was able to find value in these devastations. There is value in everything that matters. We just need to look hard, and we will find that it is always there.

March 20, 2012

I have just discovered that I am using inappropriate language, lack of patience, and is making too much noise.

I also need to stop hollering so much. I must also be careful to watch myself. If I do this, I will not fall so much.

When I gave my Lectio Divina, I learned if you are obedient to Jesus, He will guide you through your life.

March 21, 2012

Today I got up and started my office (prayer). A reading from Deuteronomy 7:6, 8–9:

The Lord, your God, has chosen you from all nations to face of the earth to be a people, particularly His own. It is because the Lord loves you, and because of His fidelity to all, He has sworn to your fathers, that He brought you out with His strong arm and from Pharaoh, king of Egypt. Understand, then, that the Lord, your God, if God indeed, the faithful God, who keeps his merciful covenant to the thousands of generations for those who love him and keep his commandments

So I have learned that if I keep the commandments of Jesus, He will never stop protecting me.

I keep hating to say this again and again. I am still not using appropriate language. I still don't have lots of patience, and I am still hollering too much. This needs to stop. I do not like to put this in my diary every day.

March 21, 2012

Okay, now what else have I done today? After saying my morning prayer, I had some breakfast. I then came back to the computer and said my Lectio Divina. Once again I learned to trust in the Lord.

I called Scott to help me put together a cabinet that Deanna and I bought for the chair in the living room.

I had a wonderful lunch that Deanna made for me. It was delicious and came with some soup.

I am trying to read a book called Little Chapel on the River. Strangely, there are many things that are in my book that relate to this book. It is about good and bad things that happen to you and shows that you should take responsibility for what you are and realize that good bad or indifferent things that happened to you, you can find great value in them. This type of thing is what I am trying to say in my book.

Yesterday, I went to see my spiritual director Mary Jo. We talked about my book. She talked about the meaning of Lent and what it has meant to me. I shared with her that the season of Lent has had a greater impact on me than ever before. It seems that the season of Lent is very rewarding to me. I am really getting the message more than ever. My daily office means more. My daily prayer means more. I am getting a greater feeling of strength and faith.

I also realize that I must share my faith. I must not be ashamed of it. I also feel verses from the Bible are just as strong and perhaps even stronger than ever before.

I have also asked Deanna who broke the door in the bathroom.

I shared with her that I was not angry about the door, but I was disappointed with the fact that she will not sell the house.

I do think that selling this house will be much better for both of us because we are not getting any younger. You do not need to take a monster like this. We would be much better off with something small just for us.

I also left a message with my publisher. I have a new submissions person who will handle my script. I left him a message on his phone, plus an e-mail. I do hope my book will work. I'm sure that it will, but I do have some reservations, but I guess that's normal. This is where my strength, prayer, and faith in Jesus comes in.

On Sunday, there was a meeting at St. Mary's Abbey in Morristown, for the Oblates. We saw a tape about a Carmelite nun, Edith Stein. She was a brilliant philosopher. To best understand her, I think you must read about her life and what she was about rather than trying to figure out what she is trying to set. Edith Stein died in Germany at a concentration camp.

Father Hillary will celebrate the anniversary of his profession (final vows). He is our leader of the Oblates.

I will now say my daytime prayer. After I do this, I'm going to rest. God bless and peace. Have a blessed day.

March 22,2012

Today I got up. As usual, I took my medication. I then said my office (morning prayer).

I learned that you should follow the Lord's will and not your own. Now I have epilepsy, I have had surgery. Therefore, from the surgery, they have cut away parts of my brain that control different parts.

Now I am not going to give the details, except these parts I will longer have. My patience, my hollering, my anxiety, my making funny noises when I fall, as you can see, I have no control over these parts of my brain. This is not a pity party. This is the way it is.

This is where I need the prayer that I may find another way so that I can control these parts. What I cannot understand is that I can acknowledge that there was a chance, then why can I not find a way to control it?

Peter just called for us to go to mass. I hope that Scott does come over to help me fix the unit I just bought. If he does not come over, then Deanna and I will fix it ourselves.

Oh, I made a terrible mistake. I spilled my breakfast all over this morning. Deanna had just finished washing the floor. I do not blame her for being very angry. The floor was not dry yet.

I will now get ready for mass.

After mass today, we did a service in the church called divine mercy.

Background of the Divine Mercy devotion:

From the diary of a Polish nun, a special devotion began spreading throughout the world in the 1930s. The message is nothing new as a reminder that the church has always thought through scripture and tradition that God is loving and forgiving and that we must show mercy and forgiveness. But in Divine Mercy devotion, the message takes a powerful new focus, calling people to a deeper understanding that God's love is unlimited and available to everyone, especially to the greatest of sinners.

The message of Divine Mercy is that God loves us in all, no matter how great our sins; that we can call upon Him, receive His mercy, and let it flow to others. Thus, all will come to share His joy. It is a message we can call to mind simply by remembering ABC: ask for mercy, be merciful, completely trust in Jesus.

So you see if I trust in Jesus no matter what, He will save me.

If I trust in the Lord, there is a purpose as to why everything in my life happened. So now if I trust in Jesus and obey Him, do you see how the good, bad or indifferent becomes bearable and significant because I have trusted in Jesus, He has given me the opportunity to see the value and be able to use this value for my life.

As I look out the window I see that we have one wonderful weather. It is like a day of spring, and it is only March.

I saw Gloria today. I have not seen her all week, and I was very concerned about her. It was not about the ride she gives me that concerns me. It was her husband that is sick. This was just as bad for her.

March 22, 2012

I shared with our organist today regarding my brain surgery. She thinks as I do that, it is something to ponder and not to understand. I must remember her name. See, there is a part of my memory, which due to my brain surgery, had been taken away.

It is also amazing today that this surgery happened many years ago, and I am still thinking about it today, but then again this is my diary. So I came home from mass to a sandwich and a bowl of soup that Deanna made, for she is an incredible person.

I have just gotten up from my nap. For some reason, I am thinking that my life has become dull. I must realize that this not really true. I must continue with prayer and build my faith, which will give me strength and make me feel useful. Deanna and I tried assembling the table that I bought for one of the chairs in the living room. However, we could not put it together ourselves, so we must get someone else to do it. I called Marion, one of the Oblates, to see if she was okay. And she said she was. Then still, we could not. We will get one of the kids across the street to do it.

March 24, 2012

Apparently, I did not communicate anything on March 23, 2012.

At the beginning, whatever I shared, for some reason, I did not keep. So let's see if I can remember. What I thought of last night were the disadvantages I have, of not being good enough for my family. I felt inadequate. I felt I was not good enough. Now you see, this is once again a pity party.

Very briefly, this is not who I am. It is just an experience I need to share so that I can get on with my life.

I must remember who I am is wonderful. I had a hearty breakfast. I also had a wondrous lunch Deanna made for me. She is also a wonderful person. I took the time to fix the Dragon writing system, but the audio would still not work, so I had to get Scott over to get it fixed. He also fixed the unit we bought. Now I have a table to use for my coffee and doughnuts on the left side so that it is more convenient for me. Because of this, I did not save my morning prayer for my Lectio Divina. As you know, this is my contemplative prayer, where you listen to a verse from the Bible and meditate on it.

Numbers 20:1–13; 21:4 29:

The whole Israelite community arrived in the desert I was in on the first of the month, and the people settled at Kadesh. Here it was that Miriam died, and here it was that she was buried.

As the community had no water, they held a council against Moses and Aaron. The people contended with Moses, exclaiming, "Why have you brought the Lord's community into the desert where we and our livestock are dying? Why did you lead us out of Egypt only to bring us into this wretched place, which has neither grain nor figs nor vines or pomegranates? Here there is not even water to drink." But Moses and Aaron went away from the assembly to the entrance of the meeting tent where they fell prostrate.

Then the glory of the Lord appeared to them, and the Lord said to Moses. "Assemble the community, you and your brother Aaron, and in their presence speak to the rock and it will pour out its waters. From the rock, you shall bring forth water for the community and their livestock to drink."

So Moses took the staff from its place before the Lord, and he was ordered. He and Aaron assembled the community in front of the rock. He said to them, "Listen to me, you rebels. Are we to bring water for you out of this rock?" Then raising his hand, Moses struck the rock twice with his staff, and the water gushed out in abundance for the community and their livestock to drink.

But the Lord said to Moses and Aaron, "Because you did not trust me to honor my sanctity before the Israelites, you shall not leave this community into the land I give them."

Now, this verse from the book of Numbers shows us that even today, we should obey and trust in Jesus. He always will give us drink and meat and will always take care of us no matter what as long as we trust in Him. You see, today, when I felt that I was inadequate with my family, Jesus showed me that if I come from who I am and not what others want, what my family thinks of the problem lies with them and not me.

As you can see, during this season of Lent, we can see how much we trust, how much we should care for others. We should treat all others as ourselves. We also have the Sacrament of Reconciliation and the Sacrament of Holy Eucharist.

I have just realized my prayer and my strength and my faith. I really realize as never before that Jesus never leaves me. I mean the feeling is so strong than ever before.

I also know that He will give me the grace to be able to finish this book. Jesus will give me the guidance I need.

I am now going to say my evening prayer. God bless and peace have a blessed day.

March 25, 2012

Well, the first thing that happened today was I lost my medical alert bracelet. Deanna looked everywhere in the bed, but the bracelet was nowhere to be found. So I decided to buy a new one, which I did.

I said my morning prayer today and it talked about being obedient to the will of God. I had a strange dream last night. It was about my mother. For some reason, she was angry with me, but I could not understand why. It was just me and not my brothers or sisters. Once again I felt that my brothers and sisters were getting away once I get in trouble. The dream was not that clear as to what it was, but as you can see again, this was another pity party that I was planning. I even do it today and it is not needed, so just stop and get on with your life, Gene.

Last night I had a terrible accident. With our new side table we bought, it is not exactly even. So as we were watching television, I knocked over cocoa all over the rug. Now, this morning we put a board under the table, and perhaps that will work for us.

This morning after coming back from church, we watched Pope Benedict say mass in Mexico. The mass was in Latin, which brought back the old days.

March 25, 2012

This morning Deanna made me a great breakfast. It was eggs, ham, juice, and coffee. As always she did a great job.

From the beginning of the letter to Hebrews 1:1 and 2:4

In times past, God spoke to our fathers through the prophets; in this, last days, He has spoken to us through His son, whom He made heir of all things and through whom also he created the universe. The sun is a reflection of the Father's glory, the exact representation of the Father's being, and He sustains all things by His powerful word.

He had claimed us from our sins. He took His seat at the right hand of the Majesty in heaven, as far to the angels as the name He has inherited is superior to theirs.

To whom of the Angels did God ever say, "You are my son to whom I have begotten you"? Then again, when He leads His firstborn into the world, He says He makes His angel's wings and His ministers' flaming fire out of the sun.

"Your throne, O God stands forever and ever; in a righteous scepter in this sector of your kingdom."

And, "Lord, of all you established the earth, and the heavens are the work of your hands. They will perish but you will remain; all of them will grow old like a garment. You will roll them up like a cloak. Like a garment they will be changed, but you are the same as you were. Years will have no end." To which of the angels has God ever said, "Lord, you have brought blessings to all mankind. Bring us to share your concern for the good of all."

May we work together to build up the earthly city, without our eyes fixed on the City that lasts forever. Healer of the body and soul, cure the sickness of our spirits, so that we may grow in holiness through your constant care.

Now as you can see, in this reading, if we bond together and help one another and respect one another, look at what can happen with our lives. If we bond together instead of being selfish, we can care and love one another and have compassion for each other. We can move mountains. We can look at what our lives can be. We can be better people. Once again, if we sacrifice ourselves for Jesus and obey Him, He will protect us and will never leave us. He is always with us no matter what we do or say.

Because of my Lectio Divina, which is my contemplative prayer, I was able to pick up on both readings and the gospel very, very clearly.

Today they had a preparation for the kids that are to receive their Confirmation. The kids had a wonderful preparation for their Confirmation. I will now say my evening prayer.

Peace, God bless and have a blessed day.

March 26, 2012

Today is the feast of the Annunciation of the Blessed Virgin Mary. This is when the angel Gabriel appeared to her, telling her that she was to be the mother of Jesus Christ. Mary was afraid, but the angel Gabriel told her not to be afraid that she was chosen by God to be the mother of Jesus.

From John 12:20–33:

The Greeks were among those who went up to worship at the festival. They came to Phillip, who was from Bathsheba in Galilee, and said to him, "Sir, we wish to see Jesus." Philip went and told Andrew, and they told Jesus, and Jesus answered them, "The hour has come for the Son of Man to be glorified truly. Truly I say to you unless a grain of wheat falls into the earth and dies, it remains alone, but if it dies it bears much fruit."

He who loves his life loses it, and he who hates his life in this world will keep it for eternal life. If anyone serves me, he must follow me, and where I am there shall be my servant be also. If anyone serves me, the Father will honor him.

Now my soul is troubled, what shall I say? "Father, save me from this hour?" No, for this purpose I have come to this hour.

Father, glorify your name! Then a voice came from heaven, "I have glorified it, and I will glorify it again."

The crowd standing by who heard it said that it must be thunder; others said an angel has spoken to Him."

Jesus answered, "This voice has come for your sake, not for mine."

Now from what has been said above, let us know that if we trust in Jesus and obey Him, he will always tell the Father how much He loves us. We must trust in Him.

Okay, now as far as what happened to me today, I was unable to go to mass, so I went online.

However, I did some things that were very inappropriate. I watched some sex and porn sites. This does not work. So I shared with Jesus and apologized to Him for having done this. However, He was with me and has told me that it was okay. "I forgive you, but see that it doesn't happen again." And He said to me, "I still love you and will never leave you. Just get on with your life."

So what I did was restore my computer from seven o'clock this morning, which was before I watched porn sex. So the sex and the porn are no longer on my computer. Jesus stayed with me and guided me, so this will not happen again.

I was able to go to mass. There was no one to pick me up. So I went online. I also helped Deanna put the groceries away. She is very, very tired, and her arms hurt her.

Jesus, please help Deanna. Please tell her that she does not have to worry about getting me my lunch. She is very, very hard on herself. She is a wonderful person. Please allow her to see this for herself.

March 26, 2012

I have just finished saying my daytime prayer.

Yesterday, I ordered a new medical ID bracelet for my epilepsy. I cannot do without it. I truly thought it was lost. Deanna and I looked high and low under the bed, in the laundry, under the chairs; it was nowhere to be seen. But then Deanna looked outside and found it on the front porch, so I called the company where I would get the bracelet and was able to cancel the order.

On Thursday I need to go to my epileptologist so he can check on the surgery I had on my brain when they took the epilepsy. I do believe that I explained it earlier in my book. You do not need to know all the medical history. The above is all you need to know.

I did have a small seizure in January. My goal is to have no seizures. I am taking my medication the way I should.

Yesterday I put in the CD everything that I have for my book so far. I also called and sent it via e-mail to Greg, who is now my publisher, to see if he would like to look at what I have done so far on the book. I also told them that this was the first time I have ever tried to write a book, so I am not sure it will work. I still have my doubts as to whether it is good or not. But I know that Jesus will never leave me. He will always, always be my guide in whatever I do. He will continue to encourage me, sell my book, and make it work. I do hope that Greg either e-mails or calls me so I know where I stand regarding this book.

Oh, I just thought that being a Benedictine oblate, I will get their prayer as they will be with me also.

I tried to talk to my friend Marion, who is also a Benedictine oblate, to see how she is. We did not get a chance to talk. She used to drive me home from the oblate meetings, but she had a heart attack, so it is not fair of me to ask her. I am more concerned about her health than I am in getting a ride home from the oblate meetings.

Our next oblate meeting is April 22, 2012. It is going to be a joint meeting with the group of Benedictine oblate sisters in Elizabeth. St. Scholastica sisters she is St. Benedict's sister also twin sister.

I just thought that now it says I am able to make CDs, that I can make them for anybody who chooses to have one. They may wish to see what the book will look like. I also need to share that there are a lot of misspelled words in my book because in the beginning, when I first wanted Dragon, I did not enunciate properly, and since that happened, the words did not come out right. I tried to correct them, but there were too many, so I left it alone. So before I give a CD out to anybody, I will tell them of the misspelled words. I am sure that my publisher Greg will call.

Okay, now I just got up from my nap. Because I cannot go out once again, I feel inadequate. I feel bad about Deanna. I am unable to take her anywhere because of my not being able to drive. She says we are going nowhere, and she is right. Okay, this is the start of another pity party. I must stop this and get on with my life.

You should never feel sorry for yourself. As you look back, you should be able to grow from that experience and become a better person. You see pity parties do not work and have no value. What you do, no matter what it is, do not ever think that it is wrong. With the help of Jesus, He will guide you through all good or bad.

Because of the fact that you are unable to drive and that you can go nowhere because of your epilepsy, that is the way it is because it is what it is. You must realize that you are the one that went through three cars and totaled them, and it is your responsibility that this has happened. Accept that, Gene. Do not blame yourself. You can never undo what has been done.

March 26, 2012

Dear Jesus, I am starting up again with this hollering, with this lack of patience, with these crazy noises. Yes, I know this probably comes from the parts that are missing in my brain from surgery, but this is no excuse. There must be a way to stop this. If I can acknowledge that all of this does happen, there must be a way to control this.

This must stop. I really need your help, Jesus, in this matter. I will continue to pray that I will have the strength of the faith to do this. Jesus, I know you can do this. It will help me because you never leave me. One more thing you must impress on Deanna that she is not required to wait for everybody else. Impress on her that she was not hired for this as she says.

Deanna does not want her name in my book, but this book is not meant to hurt her feelings or to make her feel bad. I would like her to know that she is a major part of my life, and I will always, always love her. Jesus, please help me with this. Tell her that she need not fear her name being used. I know you will help me in this matter.

After writing all this, I am now beginning to feel much better about myself, I am a better person for it.

Peace and God bless have a blessed day.

March 27, 2012

Today I got up and left. I got dressed. I said my morning office. From this point on, we are now preparing for Palm Sunday.

After sharing myself and what happened, I will share the purpose of the objective Palm Sunday.

As usual, Deanna made me a wonderful breakfast. After eating breakfast, I said my Lectio Divina. As you know, this is my contemplative prayer, the kind of prayer wherein you meditate and then concentrate on verses from the Bible.

What happened after this was I lost the crucifix that I always wear so I always think of Jesus. I think the fact that I do not drive has filled my life with prayer and has given me great strength and great faith in who I am. This is very important to me, as it makes me grow to become a better person.

I got an e-mail from my brother Jerry, asking how the hell I am doing. He is my oldest brother. He has lost his wife, Nancy, some time ago, but he is now well-adjusted. He has been always wonderful to me. He has been a great guidance for me. He has taught me how to invest my money.

Deanna has gone to wash her car. She has called Blair, a clothing store, to get some stirrup pants, but they do not make them anymore.

Deanna is now gone to the car wash. The people who own the place give her two or three car washes because she is a very good customer. She gets very angry when I am not able to get a ride to church. I do wish she would care for herself and allow herself to be who she is.

Deanna must understand that if we sell this house, we can make it easier on both of us. She says that she is tired, and her arms no longer work and other bodily things as well. If she would only realize that by selling this house, things could be so, so much better for both of us.

March 27, 2012

Part of John 12:12–16:

The next day a great crowd who had come to the feast heard that Jesus was coming to Jerusalem, so they took branches of palm trees and went out to meet Him, crying out, "How blessed is he who comes in the name of the Lord." "Blessed be the king of Israel!" and Jesus found a young donkey and sat upon it. It is written, "Fear not, daughter of Zion your King is coming, sitting on a donkey's colt." His disciples did not understand this at first, but when Jesus was glorified, they remembered this had been written of Him and had been done to Him.

Consider for a moment the excitement of the people. Many in the crowd came from Galway to celebrate the Passover of the holy city of Jerusalem.

When Jesus began His public ministry, many of them rejected both Him and His teachings. But know that when they had seen for themselves His power to heal and the truth of His teachings, they welcomed Him. Would today be the day He would emerge as the long-expected Messiah and free them from foreign domination?

Today they took palm branches out to meet Him, but why palm?

The palm branch was a symbol of triumph and victory. The Romans rewarded champions of games and celebrated military success with palm branches.

Palm branches also symbolize the victory of faithful over enemies of the soul. The people were shouting "Hosanna!" Hosanna means "please save" or "save now" (Psalms 118:25). Hosanna came to be a sign of praise. The entrance song to Psalm 118:26 was "Blessed be he who answers in the name of the Lord." It's hard to believe that in just a few days, this crown of celebration would be calling for the crucifixion of Jesus.

Now, what do you think all this means to us today? It shows our doubt even today that when things do not go our way, when we do not trust in Jesus. Isn't it strange? If we have faith in Jesus, shouldn't we show Compassion and care, support, love, and accept others? If these things are not done, we crucify Jesus. We expect what we want. If things do not go our way, we have no faith. What happens to us, good, bad, or indifferent, is all part of life. Always remember that Jesus is with us and He will never leave us.

Once again let us pray that we will have the strength, the faith, and with our Lord Jesus, we can rule mountains.

This afternoon after lunch, I went online and found this senior citizen newsletter. Deanna and I are looking for trips to go places. There were some trips in the old newsletter that went to Atlantic City. Hopefully, there will be some trips for us in their future in the newsletter. I put a shortcut on my desktop for North Plainfield Senior Citizens Club. There should be some trips and newsletters that are coming up. At least we will have the newsletter for North Plainfield and will be able to look at it regarding church.

I will now say my daytime prayer.

Peace and God bless and have a blessed day.

Glossary/ Definition of Terms:

1. **Lectio Divina** – (Latin for Divine Reading) is a traditional Benedictine practice of scriptural reading, meditation and prayer intended to promote communion with God and to increase the knowledge of God's Word. It does not treat Scripture as texts to be studied, but as the Living Word. It has been around since AD 300. It follows a four-step approach of: Reading; Meditation; Prayer; Contemplation.

2. **Benedictine Oblate** – Oblates of St. Benedict are Christian individuals or families who have associated themselves with a Benedictine community in order to enrich their Christian way of life. Oblates shape their lives by living the wisdom of Christ as interpreted by St. Benedict. Oblates seek God by striving to become holy in their chosen way of life. By integrating their prayer and work, they manifest Christ's presence in society.

3. **Muriel Siebert** – Muriel Siebert & Co., is a stock discount brokerage firm. The firm trades in municipal bonds, government agency bonds, corporate bonds, and equities.

4. **Dragon Computers** – prides itself in being able to supply whole units and parts to a worldwide customer base across the full range of equipment, remarketing, asset management, consultancy and distribution.

5. **Feast of St. Blaise** – St. Blaise is also venerated as one of the "Fourteen Holy Helpers," a group of saints invoked as early as the 12th century in Germany and who are honored. He miraculously cured a small boy who was choking to death on a fishbone lodged in his throat. By the

sixth century, St. Blaise's intercession was invoked for diseases of the throat in the East.

6. **About the Book of Job** – The prologue on earth shows the righteous Job blessed with wealth and sons and daughters. The scene shifts to heaven, where God asks Satan for his opinion of Job's piety. Satan answers that Job is pious only because God has blessed him; if God were to take away everything that Job had, then he would surely curse God. God gives Satan permission to take Job's wealth and kill all of his children and servants, but Job nonetheless praises God: "Naked I came out of my mother's womb, and naked shall I return: the Lord has given, and the Lord has taken away; blessed be the name of the Lord."

CPSIA information can be obtained
at www.ICGtesting.com
Printed in the USA
BVHW08s1326170618
519234BV00004B/23/P